Pāli

Buddha's Language

A teach-yourself course for beginners
in
10 simple lessons

By
Kurt Schmidt

Theravada Tipitaka Press

Visit our website at pali.nibbanam.com

Printed in the United States of America

1st Edition December 2009,
2nd Edition July 2011

ISBN- 978-1475229745

Contents

Introduction

There is no translation that can replace the original, simply because very often the meaning of words of one language are not fully compatible with those of another language and the sentence structure of one cannot be reproduced in the other.

Each translation therefore carries the spirit of the translator – even if it tries to be as close to the original text as possible. A translation that would be correct in every detail does not exist. In particular, any translation will be insufficient if the original (as is the case with Pāli) presents itself with linguistic beauty, richness of expression and poetic melody - characteristics which a translation will have a hard time to capture.

It is therefore desirable to anyone who wants to delve deeper into the Buddhist teachings to eventually learn the language of the Pāli canon, which is the Buddha's language[1] - Or at least to get to know it to an extant as to be able to read the more important speeches and sayings of the Buddha in the original and be able to understand them.

Previously, access to knowledge of Pāli was rather difficult, as the Pāli grammars available assumed knowledge of Sanskrit (which is a language related to Pāli) or their presentation was such that in

---

[1] According to the Theravada Buddhist tradition, Pāli was the language spoken by the Buddha. Modern research places Pāli historically and linguistically in very close proximity to the Buddhas own language - thus Pāli could have been either a dialect at the time of the Buddha or a lingua franca combination of various dialects from the first decades of Buddhism.

order to read one Pāli sentence one had to struggle through a dry scholastic grammar…

However, it is possible even without the knowledge of Sanskrit and without too much investment of time and effort to understand the Pāli texts, in such a way that the beginner will be given the opportunity, starting with the very first lesson, to get a feeling for the original Pāli canon texts. In this booklet we present a number of well organized and structured snippets of canonical and post-canonical Pāli literature. They have been organized in such a way as to help explain the grammar on the fly with a small, but for the start sufficient vocabulary which is easy to memorize. The examples from the canon are chosen so that they are in content and form suitable for memorization.

A piece from the Milindapañha was chosen as an example to highlight the diversity of style and expression between older and younger texts.

Those who complete the first nine lessons already know so much of the Pāli grammar that they will be able to understand simple texts with the help of a dictionary. The tenth lesson is just a text and list of new words.

For further studies we recommend the following books:

- A.K Warder: Introduction to Pāli
- Rune E. A. Johansson: Pāli Buddhist Texts: An Introductory Reader and Grammar
- Gair, Karunatilaka: A New Course in Reading Pāli: Entering the Word of the Buddha

Introduction to the 2nd Edition

Nearly two decades ago Markus Pesendorfer (later Ven. Paññādhamma) gave me Kurt Schmidt's small booklet entitled "Pali, Buddha's Sprache" and I was fascinated. Huddled in a bus seat one late night coming home from a Pali course in Vienna I soon enjoyed my first weeks with Pali through Kurt Schmidt's thoroughly wonderful primer. For many reasons it turned out to be the perfect jumping board into what later became a life long interest in Pali – the book was concise and to the point. It promised an achievable goal with its arrangement of fundamental Pali grammar and vocabulary in ten short chapters. It focused on the words of the Buddha – the whole reason for which I had decided to learn Pali in the first place – and finally, it emphasized memorization time and again as an important corner stone of Pali studies.

When a few years back some Buddhist friends in Florida asked me if I could teach them Pali quite naturally my first look went out to see if Kurt Schmidt's old book had been translated into English in the meantime – it had not. And so together with many Floridian Dhamma friends we created a curriculum based on the book while translating it at the same time.

Eventually the translation was completed in 2009 and published by the TheravadaTipitaka Press, a small non-profit organization supporting the Mahamevnawa Meditation Monastery – Florida's first meditative Buddhist monastery in the Sri Lankan Theravada forest tradition.

While there are quite a number of English resources for students interested in Pali, still most of them require a profound linguistic knowledge or progress slowly. It seems that Kurt Schmidt's "Pali,

Buddha's language" filled a gap between the more sophisticated Pali grammars, dictionaries and textbooks and the interested lay person who wanted to have a first quick look at some basic facts and functioning of Pali.

Over the past three years we received a lot of great feedback for this book and many valuable improvements went into the second edition. Please let us know if you have any suggestion for further editions and make sure to visit our complementary website with many audio files to supplement the exercises found in this book.

Finally thank you for your interest in this project – every dollar you have spent went into the foundation of a new spiritual place, open to all, where the very principles you will be able to uncover in the Buddha's own words are re-discovered and practiced for the benefit of all,

with Metta,

The Translator.
Theravada Tipitaka Press c/o
Mahamevnawa Meditation Monastery, Florida

Kataññutāya

To Carolyn White and Linda Fischer
for their dedication and patience

George White
for his example of "learning by osmosis"

John Allan and Jayarava
for their valuable feedback and corrections

Nadine, Ivan, Philipp, Lars, James, Jay, Renu, Jeff, Brian, Marion, Colin, Jared, Kaylee and all others whose kindness and Dhamma practice supported this project

List of Abbreviations:

acc	=	accusative case
abl	=	ablative = from, away from
abs	=	absolutivum
adj	=	adjective
adv	=	adverb
act	=	active
dat	=	dative case
Dhp	=	Dhammapada
fem	=	feminine
gen	=	genitive, possessive
intr	=	instrumental case
imp	=	imperative
caus	=	causative
loc	=	locative case
lat	=	Latin
masc	=	masculine
nom	=	nominative case
neut	=	neuter
opt	=	optative
part	=	participle
pass	=	passive
pers	=	person
pl	=	plural
pp	=	past participle
ppp	=	past participle passive
pres	=	present tense
pron	=	pronoun
skr	=	Sanskrit
sing	=	singular
ved	=	Vedic
cmp	=	compare
pre	=	prefix

First Lesson

Pāli Alphabet

The Pāli language has 42 sounds.

Of these, 8 are vowels, 34 consonants.

There is no distinct alphabet for Pāli. The most ancient alphabet that we know was used for writing Pali is called "Brahmi" and was found in inscriptions from the time of Emperor Ashoka, 260 BC (*see picture*). Some believe that this script may have already been in use during the time of the Buddha.

Today, in Asia, Pāli is written in each country's national alphabet. In Singhalese characters in Sri Lanka, in India it is mostly written in Devanagari, in Myanmar it is written in Burmese characters, in Thai letters in Thailand and in Europe and America we use the Latin alphabet.[2]

[2] See Appendix A for an overview over various scripts and Pāli characters.

However, since the Latin alphabet has only 25 letters, there are a couple of additions (diacritics) to represent the additional Pali sounds – some vowels have additional strokes on their top and some consonants can show additional dots above or underneath their letters. There are also combined letters with an additional "h" to indicate extra-aspiration.

With a dot below their letter we identify "cerebral" sounds: ṭ, ṭh, ḍ, ḍh, ṇ, ḷ and ḷh. The dots in this case indicate that you have to press your tongue against the palatal region in your mouth when pronouncing the sound. With a dot above the character we indicate guttural sounds like ṅ, which is pronounced like "n" in front of a "k" or "g", similar to English "n" in words like "si**n**k" or "si**n**g".

For nasalized vowels like **ang, ing, ung** at the end of a word (*"niggahītaṃ" in Pāli*) we use a separate vowel sign which is indicated by **ṃ**. This **ṃ** has to be pronounced like "**ng**" (as in ba**ng**, sa**ng** etc).

Pronunciation of an Indian alphabet can first seem daunting if you are not familiar with Indian languages. Please make sure to visit our website which has various audio files you can listen too and links so other online resources for proper Pali pronunciation.

Try to listen to these sound clips as often as you can, while trying to replicate the sounds as good as you can. Even better: try visiting a Sri Lankan or Indian Buddhist monastery or temple close to where you live and ask the monks if they could help you with your Pali pronunciation – as native speakers of an Indian language they will be excellent tutors and very often offer Pali courses for beginners.

The Indian alphabet - according to which most Pāli-dictionaries are organized – is quite contrary to our random Latin alphabet.

It is sorted in a phonetic manner:

Vowels:	a, ā, i, ī, u, ū, e, o	
Nasal:	ṃ	
Consonants:		

	non-sonant		sonant		nasal
	non-aspirant.	aspirant	non-aspirant	aspirant	
Gutturals	k	kh	g	gh	ṅ
Palatals	c	ch	j	jh	ñ
Cerebrals	ṭ	ṭh	ḍ	ḍh	ṇ
Dentals	t	th	d	dh	n
Labials	p	ph	b	bh	m

half-vowels and liquids (sonants) include: y, r, l, ḷ, ḷh, v, s, h

So if you have to lookup a word in a Pali dictionary make sure you remember to search for the word according to the Pali alphabet.

Pronunciation

a is pronounced like *u* in **c*u*t**
ā is pronounced like *a* in **f*a*ther**
I is pronounced like *i* in **m*i*ll**
ī is pronounced like *ee* in **b*ee***
u is pronounced like *u* in **p*u*t**
ū is pronounced like *oo* in **c*oo*l**
k is pronounced like *k* in ***k*ite**
g is pronounced like *g* in ***g*ood**
ṅ is pronounced like *ng* in **si*ng*er** (yes, there is no big difference between this and ṃ)
c is pronounced like *ch* in ***ch*ur*ch***
j is pronounced like *j* in ***j*am**
ñ is pronounced like *ñ* in Spanish **señor**
ṭ is pronounced like *t* in **ha*t***
ḍ is pronounced like *d* in **goo*d***
ṇ is pronounced like neut in ***n*ow**

Note: We recommend that you try to listen to a Sri Lankan or Indian speaker who will pronounce Pāli words and sounds in a more authentic way. You can find online resources with examples of many Pāli words and their proper pronunciation.[3]

---

[3] Please visit our website at http://pali.nibbanam.com. You will find audio files for all passages occuring in this book as free downloadable files. This way you can check your pronunciation.

Accentuation and Length

Accentuation in Pāli is weak and is defined according to the length of the penultimate syllable. If it is long then that syllable will carry the accentuation, if it is short the third syllable from the end of the word will be accentuated.

Examples: **verena** accentuation is on the penultimate syllable because of the long e; **sammanti** again accentuated on the penultimate *a* because the two consonants "nt" follow which make it a "long" syllable (though the *a* is by itself short); **kudācanaṃ** is an example for accentuation on the third syllable from the end, because the penultimate syllable is short and thus does not carry the accentuation.

Even more important than the weak accentuation is the length of a syllable: The vowels **a, i, u** have to be spoken shorter (shorter in time voicing the letter) while **ā, ī, ū** come with approximately double the time than the vowels lacking a diacritic; The short "a" is pronounced very open like "cut" while the long "ā" would sound like "father".

e, o are always long except when they are found before double consonants, in which case they are pronounced short, for instance in words like m**e**ttā, kh**e**tta, k**o**ṭṭha, s**o**tthi.

Pāli dictionaries do not show nouns and adjectives in the first case (nominative) but rather in the (un-inflected) base or stem form. The same is true for verbs: you will not find them in their infinitive forms in Pali dictionaries but rather with their root form or in their present tense 3rd person singular form (following the Indian tradition).

Pāli does not have articles. Therefore you can translate: *dhamma* as "**the** teaching" or "**a** teaching" or simply "teaching", according to context.

The copula (supporting verb) "is" and "are" is dropped in many Pāli sentences. Therefore, in your translations you will sometimes have to add "is" and "are" yourself.

Reading Exercise

Training Sentences

t o b e m e m o r i z e d!

Na hi verena verāni
Not namely through-enmity enmities
sammant' īdha kudācanaṃ
stop here ever
a-verena ca sammanti
through-non-enmity and they stop
esa dhammo sanantano.
this Law (is) eternal. (Dhp. 5)

Daṇḍen'eke damayanti
Through-stick some tame
aṅkusehi kasāhi ca
through-goads through-whips
a-daṇḍena a-satthena
By (using) no-stick, by (using) no-sword
nāgo danto mahesinā.
the elephant (was) tamed by-the-great-sage. (Cullavagga VII,3,12)

Remarks

sammant' and *daṇḍen'* lost their final vowel because the following word also started with a vowel. Such omissions are frequent in verses, less often in prose. *sammant'* stand for sammanti, *daṇḍen'* for daṇḍena.
kasāhi is *intrumental plural* of kasā *fem* ;
mahesinā is *instrumental sing* of mahesi;

More explanations follow in Lesson number two.

This Dhammapada verse belongs to a group of three double stanzas. This one contains the explanation for the two preceding ones. Therefore it starts with a "*hi*" = "namely" in order to connect with the preceding one.
The suffix **a-** (before a vowel it is **an-**) as found in words as *averena, adaṇḍena, asatthena,* expresses a negation – very similar to the English "dis-" or "un-". Such negated words do quite often have a positive meaning in Pāli. Therefore "Non-Enmity" = "Conciliation", like in English "unblemished" = "spotless".

Translation

Through enmity namely enmities will here never stop, through reconciliation can they be stopped. This law is eternal.
Some tame with sticks, goads or whips.

Without stick and without weapon did the great sage tame the elephant.

Vocabulary

sammati » √ sam = to calm down	**damayati** » √ dam = tame
danta *ppp* of √ dam = tam**ed**	**vera** *neut* = the enmity
daṇḍa *masc* = the stick, club, bar, punishment	**aṅkusa** *masc* = the goad, prick
sattha *neut* = the weapon, sword	**kudācanaṃ** = ever
esa *masc* = this	**eke** *masc pl* = some (from eka, one)
sanantana = eternal	**na** = not
hi = namely	**ca** = and (placed behind a word)
dhamma *masc* = law, order, justice, truth, teaching, thing	
nāga *masc* = the (strong) elephant, snake(-goddess)	

Grammar

a- Declension

Masculine and neuter nouns which end in **-a** in their stem forms (for instance: dhamm**a**, nāg**a**, daṇḍ**a**, aṅkus**a** or neuter words such as: ver**a**, satth**a**) are declined as follows:

	Singular		*Plural*	
	Masc.	*Neuter*	*Masc.*	*Neuter*
Nom	dhammo	veraṃ	dhammā	verāni (-ā)
Gen	dhammassa	verassa	dhammānaṃ	verānaṃ
Dat	dhammassa	verassa	dhammānaṃ	verānaṃ
Aacc	dhammaṃ	veraṃ	dhamme	verāni (-e)
Instr	dhammena	verena	dhammehi	verehi
Abl	dhammā	verā	dhammehi	verehi
Loc	dhamme	vere	dhammesu	veresu
Voc	dhamma	vera	dhammā	verāni

*Adjectives, which end in **-a*** will be declined in exactly the same way (according to the noun they are grouped with), e.g.: sanantano, sanantanassa, sanantanassa, sanantanaṃ, sanantanena, sanantanā, sanantane, and so forth.

The a-declension is fundamental to learning and understanding Pāli. We recommend you learn the a-declensions by heart before proceeding. The a-declensions is the most common declension in Pāli. Please refer to Appendix B if you need more information on cases and how they work.

Conjugation of verbs

Present tense of active verbs

Most verbs form their so called **stem** by adding **-a** oder **-ya** or **-aya** to their **root**, while the -y will get assimilated with the last consonant of the root.

Examples: √ sam + ya = (stem) samma; √ dam + aya = (stem) damaya

Now, in order to get the proper conjugated verb, we attach certain suffixes at the end of the stem:

	Sing	*pl*
1. person	**-mi**	**-ma**
2. person	**-si**	**-tha**
3. person	**-ti**	**-nti**

Only exception being that before the -**mi** and -**ma** the a of the a-stem will be lengthened into an **ā in the first person singular and plural**.

Therefore, we conjugate the verbs of the present tense thus:

samm<u>āmi</u>	I calm down	**damay<u>āmi</u>**	I tame
samm<u>asi</u>	You calm down	**damay<u>asi</u>**	You tame
samm<u>ati</u>	He, she, it calms down	**damay<u>ati</u>**	He, she, it tames
samm<u>āma</u>	We calm down	**damay<u>āma</u>**	We tame
samm<u>atha</u>	You calm down	**damay<u>atha</u>**	You tame
samm<u>anti</u>	They calm down	**damay<u>anti</u>**	They tame

Reading and memorization exercise

Na hi verena verāni sammant' idha kudācanaṃ
averena ca sammanti, esa dhammo sanantano.

Daṇḍen' eke damayanti aṅkusehi kasāhi ca,
adaṇḍena asatthena nāgo danto mahesinā.

Quick recap: cases
How to interpret cases of Pali nouns

> Please refer to **Appendix B** for a more detailed introduction to some of the more important grammatical basics.

To know how to use and translate cases and conjugation is sometimes confusing for someone who never studied a classical language before.
Below are some declension and conjugation examples if you just need a quick recap. If you need more help, please read Appendix B first before you proceed.

Nominative Case:
Indicates the subject of a sentence.

Buddh**o** gacchati.
The Buddha goes. [*Who* goes? The Buddha goes.]

Accusative Case:
Indicates the object of an activity

Ahaṃ Buddh**aṃ** passāmi.
I see *the Buddha*. [*Whom* do I see?]

Possessive Case:
Indicates that something belongs to someone

Buddh**assa** kutim gacchasi.
You go to the house *of the Buddha*. [*Whose* house?]

Dative Case:
Indicates that something is for someone (indirect object)

Dhammo Buddh**assa** satthā hoti.
The Dhamma is a teacher *for the Buddha* [*For whom*?]

Instrumental Case:
Indicates a tool, instrument by which something is done.

Buddh**ena** upasikā kathenti.
The Upasikas talk *with the Buddha*. [*With whom*?]

Ablative Case:
Indicates that something comes from something or someone

Buddh**ato** dhammaṃ uganhātha.
You (plural) learn the Dhamma from the Buddha. [*From Whom*?]

Locative Case:
Indicates a location or relationship

Buddh**e** saddhaṃ labhāma.
We develop faith in the Buddha (or: on account of) [*Where? On account of/with regard to what?*]

This is just a basic and quick recap. Please check Appendix B for an in depth discussion of these important grammatical terms.

The Verb – Present Tense Summary & Examples

Buddh**o** gacchati. ⇨ Buddh**ā** gacchanti.
(The Buddha goes ⇨ The Buddhas go).
Buddh**aṃ** passāmi. ⇨ Buddh**e** passāmi
(I see the Buddha => I see the Buddhas).
Buddh**assa** ārāmaṃ gacchasi. ⇨ Buddh**ānaṃ** ārāmaṃ gacchasi.
(Go to the monastery of the Buddha ⇨ Go to the monastery of the Buddhas)
Dhammo Buddh**assa** satthā hoti
⇨ Dhammo Buddh**ānaṃ** satthā hoti. Dhamma is the teacher of the Buddha(s)
Buddh**ena** upāsikā kathenti. ⇨ Buddh**ehi** upāsikā kathenti. The lay devotes talk with the Buddha(s)
Buddh**ato** dhammaṃ uganhātha. ⇨ Buddh**ehi** dhammaṃ ugaṇhātha. You learn the Dhamma from the Buddha(s)
Buddh**e** saddham labhāma. ⇨ Buddh**esu** saddhaṃ labhāma. We develop faith in the Buddha(s).

The above examples show the usage of several verbs in *singular* and *plural* applying different cases. Below, as a summary, we conjugate *"gacchati"* to show all possible persons (of the present tense) in one place:

ahaṃ gehaṃ gacch**āmi**
I go to the house.
tvaṃ gehaṃ gacch**asi**
You go to the house.
so/sā/taṃ gehaṃ gacch**ati**
He/She/It goes to the house.

mayaṃ gehaṃ gacch**āma**
We go to the house
tumhe gehaṃ gacch**atha**
You go to the house
te gehaṃ **gacchanti**
They go to the house

These are all the possible verb conjugations for the present tense. This little table also includs the personal pronouns (i.e. words like *I, you, they,* etc.) which you will learn more about in lesson six.

The word *"geha"* meaning "house" is a noun of the a-declension (it ends in –a in its stem form). It is the object of our sentence ("to the house", i.e. the target of our movement) which therefore acts as an object of our sentence and becomes geh**aṃ** indicated by the accusative case (*singular*).

Second Lesson

Training Sentences

t o b e m e m o r i z e d!

Na jaṭāhi na gottena
Not by means of mated-hair not by means of family
na jaccā hoti brāhmaṇo
not by means of caste is (someone) a Brahmin
yamhi saccañ ca dhammo
by whom truth and justice
ca so sucī so ca brāmaṇo.
as well as pure this one a Brahmin (is).
(Dhp 393)

Udakaṃ hi nayanti nettikā
The water namely direct the well builder,
usukārā namayanti tejanaṃ
the arrowsmiths bend the arrow
dāruṃ namayanti tacchakā
the wood bend the carpenters,
attānaṃ damayanti paṇḍitā.
oneself tame the wise. (Dhp 80)

Sabbe saṅkhārā aniccā
All fabrications are impermanent
ti yadā paññāya passati
so when through wisdom he sees,

atha nibbindatī dukkhe
then he gets weary of suffering.
esa maggo visuddhiyā.
this (is) the path to purity. (Dhp 277)

Sabbe saṅkhārā dukkhā ti yadā paññāya passati
atha nibbindatī dukkhe esa maggo visuddhiyā. (Dhp 278)

Sabbe dhammā anattā ti yadā paññāya passati
atha nibbindatī dukkhe esa maggo visuddhiyā. (Dhp 279)

Remarks

jaccā is a contraction of **jātiyā**.
due to the rhythm of the verse the **i** was dropped ("metri causa"). The remaining **ty** sounds exactly like a **cc**. This explains the difference in orthography.

In **saccañ ca** you can see how the ending **ṃ** was changed because of the following **c** and became a palatal **ñ**. Try saying " ṃca" and you will hear that it turns quite naturally into a sound which is more precisely transcribed with "ñca".

sucī is *neut sing* of **sucin**.
attānaṃ is *accusative* of **attan**. Explanation of both these words and forms in the next lesson, lesson 3.
ti or **iti** defines the end of a quote or an object clause and has the same meaning as our " " (quotation marks) and -

does not have to be translated.[4] Pali does not have an indirect speech and thus every thought or spoken word is quoted with "iti". In English such a grammatical structure (*"be like quotative"*) is found as well, especially in colloquial usage; for example: "And I thought like 'wow, this is for me'."

In **nibbindatī** the final **i** was lengthened to fit the verse rhythm.

anattā is *neut sing* of the noun **an-attan** (explanation see. 3rd lesson). This is important! Therefore it does not mean: All things are void of being (*adjective pl*), but rather: All things are not the self, not the I (*noun sing*).

Translation:

Not through mated hair nor through family relation,
nor through ones caste does one become a Brahmin.
Who is endowed with truth and justice,
He is pure, he is a Brahmin.

Water is directed by those who build wells,
Arrowsmiths bent arrows,
Wood is being bent by carpenters,
Their self do the wise ones tame.

(*word pun*: nayanti, namayanti, damayanti)

All fabrications are impermanent.

---

[4] See http://theravadin.wordpress.com/2008/03/28/iti-and-sallakkheti/ and http://staefcraeft.blogspot.com/2010/09/english-like-can-like-function-like.html for a discussion on iti and how to render it in English.

Who sees this with wisdom,
will get weary of suffering.
This is the path to purification.
All fabrications are unsatisfying. Who ...
All things are not a self. Who ...

Vocabulary

nayati √ nī = to lead – this verb extends the √ -vowel ī to aya
namayati √ nam = to bow, to bend
passati √ pas = to see
nibbindati √ vid + prefix nir- = find-away, become disenchanted, become weary of (with *locative* !)
The root **√ vid** becomes vind in the stem form; **r** + **v** = become **bb**;

bhavati (hoti) √ bhū = to be, become. the **ū** of the √ is being extended to **ava** when the stem is formed. **hoti** is a very frequent alternative form of this verb – here the **bh** has been reduced to **h** and **ava** contracted to **o**, thus **hoti**.

gotta *neut* = family	**dukkha** *neut* = suffering, pain
brāhmaṇa *masc* = Brahmin	**dukkha** (*adj*) = unsatisfying, painful
sacca *neut* = truth	**sucin** (*adj*) = pure
nettika *masc*= well builder	**tejana** *neut* = arrow

eso, esa, so *masc* = this	**taccaka** *masc* = carpenter
sabbe *plural* = all	**paṇḍita** *masc* = wise man, learned man
atha = then	**yadā** = if, then
attan *masc* = the I, the self, the soul	**an-attan** *masc* = the Non-Self
udaka *neut* = water	**magga** *masc* = the path
usukārā *m* = arrowsmith	**visuddhi** *f* = purity
a-nicca = im-permanent, not eternal	**nicca** = eternal, persisting
ca - ca (placed after a word) = as well as	

Grammar

i- and u- Declension:

Nouns of this declension which end in -i or -u are masculine (e.g. agg**i** = fire, bhikkh**u** = monk) or neuter (e.g. dār**u** = wood, akkh**i** = eye).

	singular		*plural*	
N	aggi	bhikkhu	aggayo, aggī	bhikkhavo, bhikkhū
G+D	aggino	bhikkhuno	aggīnaṃ	bhikkhūnaṃ
A	aggiṃ	bhikkhuṃ	aggayo, aggī	bhikkhavo, bhikkhū
I+Ab	agginā	bhikkhunā	aggīhi	bhikkhūhi
L	aggismiṃ,	bhikkhusmiṃ,	aggīsu	bhikkhūsu
	aggimhi,	bhikkhumhi		
	aggini			

Neuter nouns which end in i- and u- have two forms in the *neut sing,* in the *accusative sing* and in the *neuter pl* und *accusative plural:*

	singular	*Plural*
N A	akkhi, akkhiṃ	akkhīni, akkhī
N A	dāru, dāruṃ	dārūni, dārū

Other than that they are declined exactly like their *masculine* counterparts.

ā- und i- Declension

Nouns which end in -ā or -i are *feminine*.
(e.g. **jaṭā** = mated hair, **jāti** = birth, caste)

	Singular		*Plural*	
N	jaṭā	jāti	jaṭā, jaṭāyo	jātī, jātiyo
G	jaṭāya	jātiyā	jaṭānaṃ	jātīnaṃ
D	jaṭāya	jātiyā	jaṭānaṃ	jātīnaṃ
A	jaṭaṃ	jātiṃ	jaṭā, jaṭāyo	jātī, jātiyo
I	jaṭāya	jātiyā	jaṭāhi, jaṭābhi	jātīhi, jātībhi
Ab	jaṭāya	jātiyā	jaṭāhi, jaṭābhi	jātīhi, jātībhi
L	jaṭāya, jaṭāyaṃ	jātiyā, jātiyaṃ	jaṭāsu	jātīsu
V	jaṭe	jāti	jaṭā	jātī, jātiyo

Feminine nouns which end in **-ī , -u** or **-ū** are declined in exactly the same way.

Declension of pronouns

Relative pronoun **yo** = …,which…
Interrogative pronoun **ko** = who?

	Singular			*plural*		
	m	*f*	N	M	*f*	N
N	yo	yā	yaṃ	ye	yā	yāni
G	yassa	yassā	yassa	yesaṃ	yāsaṃ	yesaṃ
D	yassa	yassā	yassa	yesaṃ	yāsaṃ	yesaṃ
A	yaṃ	yaṃ	yaṃ	ye	yā	yāni
I	yena	yāya	Yena	yehi	yāhi	yehi
Ab	yasmā	yāya	yasmā	yehi	yāhi	yehi
	yamhā		yamhā			
L	yasmiṃ	yassaṃ	yasmiṃ	yesu	yasu	yesu
	yamhi		yamhi			

ko (who?) has in its neuter form and in its accusative declension: **kiṃ** (what?) no plural. Other than that it is declined exactly like **yo**.

From the declension of pronouns the suffixes **-asmā** and -**amhā** of the ablative case and **-asmiṃ** and -**amhi** of the locative case entered the noun and adjective declension of masculine and neuter nouns.

Therefore, besides *ablative* **dhammā** we can also find **dhammasmā** and **dhammamhā**; besides *ablative* **verā** we can also find **verasmā** and **veramhā**, besides *locative*

dhamme also **dhammasmiṃ** and **dhammamhi**, and besides *locative* **vere** we can also find **verasmiṃ** and **veramhi**, as well as **aggismā, aggimhā, bhikkhusmā, bhikkhumhā**.

Reading exercise

Na jaṭāhi na gottena na jaccā hoti brāhmaṇo,
yamhi saccañ ca dhammo ca sucī so ca brāhmaṇo. (Dhp 293)

Udakaṃ hi nayanti nettikā, usukārā namayanti tejanaṃ,
dāruṃ namayanti tacchakā, attānaṃ damayanti paṇḍitā. (Dhp 80)

Sabbe saṅkhārā aniccā ti yadā paññāya passati,
atha nibbindatī dukkhe, esa maggo visuddhiyā. (Dhp 277)

Sabbe saṅkhārā dukkhā ti yadā paññāya passati,
atha nibbindatī dukkhe, esa maggo visuddhiyā. (Dhp 278)

Sabbe dhammā anattā ti yadā paññāya passati,
atha nibbindatī dukkhe, esa maggo visuddhiyā. (Dhp 279)

Third Lesson

Training Sentences

to be memorized!

Namo tassa bhagavato arahato sammāsambuddhassa!
Veneration to him, the Blessed One, the Holy One, the fully complete Awakened One!
Buddhaṃ saraṇaṃ gacchāmi
To the Buddha to the refuge i go
Dhammaṃ saraṇaṃ gacchāmi
To the Teaching to the refuge I go
Saṅghaṃ saraṇaṃ gacchāmi
To the community to the refuge I go

Dīghā jāgarato ratti,
Long (is) for-the-wake-person the night,
dīghaṃ santassa yojanaṃ
Long to-the-tired-one the mile
dīgho bālānaṃ saṃsāro
Long to-the-unwise the journey (in samsara),
saddhammaṃ avijānataṃ.
(for) the true-teaching not-knowing-one.

Divā tapati ādicco, rattiṃ ābhāti candimā,
During the day burns the sun, during the night shines the

moon,
sannaddho khattiyo tapati, jhāyī tapati brāhmaṇo,
with (his) weapons the warrior blazes, meditating blazes the brahmin,
atha sabbaṃ aho-rattiṃ buddho tapati tejasā.
but day and night does the Buddha blaze by his glory.
Idha nandati pecca nandati
Here happy is and after death happy is
kata-puñño ubhayattha nandati
having done merit in both happy (he) is
puññaṃ me katan' ti nandati
I have done merit, thus he is happy
bhiyyo nandati suggatiṃ gato.
but more so is happy who to heaven has gone.

Remarks

namo is *nominative* of **namas** = Bowing down, showing respect; it is derived from √ nam = to bow, bend, to venerate.
nama is one of the few stems ending in **-s** , the same as the stem **tejas** (neuter) = Shining, fire, blaze, energy, power;
me is the personal pronoun of the first person in the instrumental/ablative case = through me, by me, from me.
katan ti stand for **kataṃ ti**. The niggahītaṃ **ṃ** is changed into the nasal sound of the dental group of letters because it is followed by a "t".
saddhamma is a composite word made from **sat**, *(past*

participle of) √ **as** (same as in latin.: esse) = to be, - therefore it means: being, really, real, good, + dhamma = the teaching, therefore translated as: the real or good teaching, e.g. the Buddha-Teaching.

Translation

Homage to Him, the Exalted One, the Worthy One, The Supremely Enlightened One.

I take my refuge to the Buddha, the Teaching and the (monastic/noble) Community.

Long is the night for one awake, Long is a league to one exhausted, Long is samsara to the childish ones Who know not the true dhamma.

The sun is bright by day, the moon enlightens the night, armored shines the warrior, contemplative the Brahmin True. But all day and night-time too resplendent does the Buddha shine.

Here one's glad, one's glad hereafter, in both ways is the merit-maker glad; 'Merit I've made', serenely one is glad, and more one is glad passed to blissful states.

Vocabulary

ābhāti from √ **bhā** = to shine on, + with prefix ā (on, towards)	
gacchati √ **gam** = to go, *past participle passive (ppp) is* **gata** = gone	**ādicca** *m* = Sun
gati *f* = the going	**canda** *f* = moon
su-gati *f* = the good path, going	**khattiya** *m* = Warrior(-caste)
teja neuter (*skr* **tejas**) = Blaze, Fire	**tapati** √ **tap** = shine
dīgha = long	**jāgarant** = being wake, wakeful
nandati √ **nand** = to be happy	**a-vijānant** = not-knowing
saṅgha *m* = Community	**saraṇa** neuter = refuge
puñña neuter = a good deed, merit	**puñña** = good, meritorious
divā = the day	**kata** *ppp* of √ **kar** = made, done
ratti *f* = the night	**ahoratti** *f* = day and night
bhiyyo = more, even more	**pecca** = after death
bāla *m* = the foolish person	**sannaddha** = having weapons
yojana neuter= one mile	**sabba** = whole, all, everyone
jhāyin = meditating	**sabbe** *pl* = all

ubhaya, ubho = both	**ubhayattha** = in both cases
santa *ppp* = tired, wearied	**bhagavat** *m* = the Blessed One, the Lucky one
buddha √ budh = awake; *Voc* = the Awakened One, + prefix **sam-** = full, complete, + prefix **sammā**	

There are three meanings for **santa** in Pali: 1. *adjective pp* (past participle) of **sammati** = silent, peaceful,i.e. calmed down (from *vedic* **śāntā**) 2. *adjective pp* of **sammati** = tired (from *vedic* **śrāntā**). It can also be seen as a form of **sant** *adj participle* of **atthi (*ved* sāt**) = being, existing, or also figurative good, real, worth, true.)

n- Declension

Nouns which have a stem ending in **-an** or **-in** are masculine words. Adjectives and Participles, whose masculine stem also ends in **-in** are declined in the same way (see example of **attan** below).

Examples:

rāja = King; (irregular Declension!),
attan *m* = The soul, the self, the „I" except used in the neuter case **atta(n)** very often has the meaning of "oneself".
suci *Adj* = pure, clean, blank; as *m* = the purity

	Singular		*plural*	
N	rājā	attā	rājāno, rājā	attāno
G+D	rājino, raññо	attano	rājūnaṃ, raññaṃ	attānaṃ, attanaṃ
A	rājānaṃ	attānaṃ, attaṃ	rājāno, rājano	attāno, attano
I	rājinā, raññā	attanā	rājūhi	attanehi, attehi
Ab	raññā	attanā	rājūhi	attanehi, attehi
L	rājini, raññi	attani	rājūsu	attanesu

In general, the *dative case is very often used for the question*: for what purpose, for what matter?
In this case it very often uses the dative ending of the the a-Declension which is **-āya**.
Examples: **atthāya** = for the benefit of, in the interest of
hitāya = for the welfare of
sukhāya = for the happiness of.

nt- Declension

Adjectives and present participles whose stem ends in **-nt** have several alternative forms in their declension table. Besides the original forms of the **–nt**-Declension many

forms of the a-Declension can be seen, which makes the nt-declension sometimes look like ending in **-nta**.
For example: **sīlavant (sīlavat)** = virtuous, moral
gacchant = going (suffix is **-nta, -ntī, -ntā** depending on gender of the word aligned with)

	singular	*plural*
N	sīlavā, sīlavanto	sīlavanto, sīlavantā
G	sīlavato, sīlavantassa	sīlavantaṃ, sīlavantānaṃ
D	sīlavato, sīlavantassa	sīlavantaṃ, sīlavantānaṃ
A	sīlavantaṃ	sīlavanto, sīlavante
I	sīlavatā, sīlavantena	sīlavantehi
Ab	sīlavatā, sīlavantā	sīlavantehi
L	sīlavati, sīlavante	sīlavantesu
N	gacchaṃ, gacchanto	gacchanto, gacchantā
G	gacchato, gacchantassa	gacchataṃ, gacchantānaṃ
D	gacchato, gacchantassa	gacchataṃ, gacchantānaṃ
A	gacchantaṃ	gacchanto, gacchante
I	gacchatā, gacchantena	gacchantehi
Ab	gacchatā, gacchantā	gacchantehi
L	gacchati, gacchante	gacchantesu

arahat (*ved* ārhat) = Holy One, is in the *neuter sing* **arahaṃ** and **arahā**, which means that this word is either declined as a participle and sometimes like an adjective. Originally it comes from the present participle of √ **araha (*skr* arha)** = morally worth, earned respect, worth, appropriate.

The feminine form of adjectives and participles ending in **-ant** are these: **-atī** or **-antī** and follow in their declension the nouns of the i-Declension.

The neuter words in *singular* and *Accusative singular end in* **-aṃ** or -**antaṃ**, in their plural form they end in **-anti or -antāni.**

Declension of the demonstrative pronouns

stem is *ta-* = he, she, it or this (masculine, feminine, neuter)

	Singular		
	m	*f*	*N*
N	so	sā	taṃ
G+D	tassa	tassā	tassa
A	taṃ	taṃ	taṃ
I	tena	tāya	tena
Ab	tamhā, tasmā	tāya	tamhā, tasmā
L	tamhi, tasmiṃ	tassaṃ	tamhi, tasmiṃ

	Plural		
	m	*f*	*N*
N	te	tā	tāni
G+D	tesaṃ	tāsaṃ	tesaṃ
A	te	tā	tāni
I	tehi	tāhi	tehi
Ab	tehi	tāhi	tehi
L	tesu	tāsu	tesu

For **taṃ** we often find **tad** if the following word starts with a vowel. The genetive (possessive case) and dative case of the feminine singular can also be **tāya**, in the plural also **tāsānaṃ**. The masculine and neuter forms in G and D plural can also show this alternative form: **tesānaṃ**.

Reading exercise

Namo tassa bhagavato arahato sammāsambuddhassa!
Buddhaṃ saraṇaṃ gacchāmi, Dhammaṃ saraṇaṃ gacchāmi,
Saṅghaṃ saraṇaṃ gacchāmi.

Dīghā jāgarato ratti, dīghaṃ santassa yojanaṃ,
dīgho bālānaṃ saṃsāro saddhammaṃ avijānataṃ. (Dhp 60)

Divā tapati ādicco, rattiṃ ābhāti candimā,
sanaddho khattiyo tapati, jhāyī tapati brāhmaṇo,
atha sabbaṃ ahorattiṃ buddho tapati tejasā. (Dhp 387)

Idhā nandati pecca nandati kata-puñño ubhayattha nandati,
puññaṃ me katan'ti nandati, bhiyyo nandati suggatiṃ gato. (Dhp 18)

Fourth Lesson

Training Sentences

Rājā āha: Bhante Nāgasena, yo uppajjati
The King said: Sir Nāgasena, who reappears,
so eva so udāhu añño ti? Thero āha:
he so he or another?" The Elder said:
na ca so na ca añño ti. Opammaṃ karohīti.
neither he nor another". „A simile make".
Taṃ kiṃ maññasi, mahārāja, yadā tvaṃ daharo
That what you think, Great King, when you a toddler
taruṇo, mando, uttānaseyyako ahosi so yeva tvaṃ
a weakling, a tenderling, a back-laying one you were he so you (was)
etarahi mahanto ti? Na hi bhante, añño so daharo
now an adult?" „No Sir, another this little child
taruṇo mando uttānaseyyako ahosi, añño
the weakling, the tenderling, the back-lying one was, another
ahaṃ etarahi mahanto ti. Evaṃ sante kho
I now (am) an adult. When that is the case now
mahārāja mātā ti pi na bhavissati, pitā ti pi
Greatking „mother" so also not will be, „father" so too
na bhavissati, ācariyo ti pi na bhavissati, sippavā
will not be, „teacher" so too will not be, „educated"
ti pi na bhavissati, sīlavā ti pi na bhavissati,
so too will not be, „virtuous" so too will not be,

paññavā ti pi na bhavissati. kin nu kho mahārāja
"wise" so too will not be. What now, oh Greatking,
aññā eva kalalassa mātā aññā abbudassa
another then the fetus' mother, another the later fetus'
mātā aññā pesiyā mātā, aññā ghanassa mātā
mother, another the embryo's mother, another the born child's mother
aññā khuddakassa mātā aññā mahantassa mātā
another the toddler's mother, another the adult's mother
aññā sippaṃ sikkhati, añño sikkhito bhavati,
another (who) the science studies, another (who) is the trained one,
añño pāpakammaṃ karoti, aññassa hathapādā
another (who) the bad-deed does, another (whom) hand&feet
chijjantī 'ti. Na hi bhante tvaṃ pana bhante
they cut apart." "No Sir, you but Sir
evaṃ vutte kiṃ vadeyyāsī 'ti. Thero āha:
after having said this, what would you say". The Elder said:
ahañ ñeva kho mahārāja daharo ahosiṃ taruṇo mando
I even, o Greatking (was) the weakling, the tenderling
uttānaseyyako ahañ ñeva etarahi mahanto imañ ñeva
the back-lying one, I even now, the adult – this very
kāyaṃ nissāya sabbe te ekasaṃgahītā 'ti.
body based on, all these are bound together.

Remarks

ti see 2nd lesson! When *a vowel* precedes the **ti** or **iti** it is lengthened as it merges with the initial **i** in **iti**.
Thera, the Elder, is the title of a monk who is at least fully ordained (a **bhikkhu**) for ten years.
kin nu: the **ṃ** of **kiṃ** is being assimilated with the following **n**.
yeva: after vowels and niggahītaṃ (i.e. the **ṃ**) the **eva** which starts with a vowel gets an **y**-prefix. Now the **ahaṃ yeva** assimilates further due to the ṃ to a **ñ** =>**ahañ ñeva**. These rules are based on Pali pronounciation rules and have no impact on grammar.
ekasaṃgahīta is a compound from **eka** = one + prefix **sam** + **gahīta**, which is a past participle (abbreviated as *ppp*) of the verb root **√ gah** = grab, therefore: being grabbed together as one.

Translation

The king said: 'He who is born, Nâgasena, does he remain the same or become another?' 'Neither the same nor another.' 'Give me an illustration.' 'Now what do you think, O king? You were once a baby, a tender thing, and small in size, lying flat on your back. Was that the same as you who are now grown up?' 'No. That child was one, I am another.' 'If you are not that child, it will follow that you have had neither mother nor father, no! nor teacher. You cannot have been taught either learning, or behaviour, or wisdom. What, great king! is the mother of the embryo in the first stage different from the mother of the embryo in the second stage, or the third, or the fourth? Is the mother of the baby a different person from the mother of the grown-up man? Is the person who goes to school one, and the same when he has finished his schooling another? Is it one who commits a crime, another who is punished by having his hands or feet cut off?' 'Certainly not. But what would you, Sir, say to that? 'The Elder replied: 'I should say that I am the same person, now I am grown up, as I was when I was a tender tiny baby, flat on my back. For all these states are included in one by means of this body.'

Vocabulary

maññati √ man = to mean, think	**ghana** *m* = embryo (just prior to birth)
sikkhati √ sikkh = train, learn	**kalala** neut = embryo (first few months)
bhante = Sir, Venerable	**pesi** *f* = fetus
ācariya *m* = teacher	**abbuda** neut = fetus
opamma neut = simile, metaphor	**khuddaka** *m* = baby
pitar *m* = father	**mātar** *f* = mother
mahant / mahā = big	**khuddaka** = little, small
sippa neut = art, science	**pana** = but
hattha *m* = hand	**pāda** *m* = foot
hatthapāda *m pl* = hands and feet	**hi** = because, namely
pañña *f* = wisdom	**paññavant** = wise

dahara = young, small	**taruṇa** = tender, fresh, new, young child
manda = small, helpless, weak	**evaṃ** = so, in this way, thus
yadā = when (time)	**kiṃ** = what? (often not translated)
udāhu = or	**kho** = now
kamma neut = deed, activity	**pi** (following a word) = and, also
kāya *m* = body	**eka** = one
na ca ... na ca = neither ... nor	**vutta** *ppp* from **√ vac** = said
uttāna = on the back lying	**seyyaka** = laying, sleeping
tvaṃ = you	**ahaṃ** = I
santa = being (see. 3rd lesson)	**eva, yeva** = emphatic part "so, even, just"; very freq. in all contexts & combns.
sīla neut = virtue, moral habit	**sīlavant** = virtuous
pāpa = bad, mean	**añña** = (an) other
nu = affirm. -- indef. part. "then, now."	
uppajjati √ pad = come to be, (re-)born	
chindati √ chid = cut, split, cut apart	
nissāya = based on, through, because of, dependent on, by means of	

Declension of the indicative pronoun

Stems are **ima** and **a** = "this"

Singular			
	masc	*fem*	*neuter*
N	ayaṃ	ayaṃ	idaṃ, imaṃ
G+D	imassa, assa	imissā, assā	imassa, assa
A	imaṃ	imaṃ	idaṃ, imaṃ
I	iminā, anena	imāya	iminā, anena
Ab	imasmā, imamhā, asmā	imāya	imasmā, imamhā, asmā
L	imasmiṃ, imamhi, asmiṃ	imāyaṃ	imamhi, asmiṃ
Plural			
N	ime	imā	imāni
G+D	imesaṃ	imāsaṃ	imesaṃ
A	ime	imā	imāni
I+Ab	imehi	imāhi	imehi
L	imesu	imāsu	imesu

Declension of nouns of relationships *(their stem ends in)* ***–r***

For example words like:

mātar = mother
pitar = father
bhātar = brother
dhītar = daughter

	singular	*plural*
N	mātā	mātaro
G+D	mātu, mātuyā	mātūnaṃ
A	mātaraṃ	mātaro
I	mātarā	mātūhi
Ab	mātarā, mātuyā	mātūhi
L	mātari	mātūsu

Also nouns which indicate activities and professions are declined in a similar way, for example:

satthar = teacher
dātar = donor
sotar = hearer
ñātar = knower

A new verb form: The „locativus absolutus"

The locative declension of a participle is used to express an activity which either preceded the activity of the main sentence or happens at the same time. We translate this construct with: "when, because of that, after that, at the same time. Examples:
evaṃ sante = in the so being; i.e. if it is so, when that is the case;
evaṃ vutte = in the so said ; i.e. when or after someone has said so

Another verb form: The FUTURE

It is very easy to create the future verb form in Pāli. One simply has to add **-iss** to the stem of the present tense verb and then attaches the same suffixes for each person as in the present tense. Here some examples:

bhavissāmi = I will be.

	singular	*plural*
1. person	bhavissāmi	bhavissāma
2. person	bhavissasi	bhavissatha
3. person	bhavissati	bhavissanti

The past tense in Pali, the "AORIST"

This is the past tense in Pāli, used when telling something which happened in the past, when relating a story. It will be enough in the beginning to simply learn a few frequent forms as the aorist construction is very irregular.

ahosiṃ = I was
ahosi = he, she, it was
āha = he, she, it said
āhu = they said

The Imperative verb form

This verb form is used to express a command.

	singular	*plural*
2. Person	gacchāhi, gaccha	gacchatha
3. Person	gacchatu	gacchantu
In the same way: karohi = make! karotha = make (plural)!		

The "Optativ" verb form

This verb form is used to express a wish or a possibility, for example **vadeyyaṃ** = I may/could say.

While the future uses the infix *–iss-* to denote future forms, the Optative uses **–eyy-** to express the "possibility" or "wish".

	singular	*plural*
1. person	vadeyy**aṃ**	vadeyyāma
2. person	vadeyy**āsi**, vad**e**	vadeyyātha
3. person	vadeyyāti, vadeyya	vadeyy**uṃ**

Reading exercise

Rājā āha: Bhanta Nāgasena, so uppajjati so eva so udāhu añño ti.
Thero āha: na ca so na ca añño ti. Opammaṃ karohī'ti.
Taṃ kiṃ maññasi mahārāja, yadā tvaṃ daharo taruṇo mando uttāna-seyyako ahosi, so yeva tvaṃ etarahi mahanto ti.
Na hi bhante, añño so daharo taruṇo mando uttānaseyyako ahosi, añño ahaṃ etarahi mahanto ti.
Evaṃ sante kho mahārāja mātā ti pi na bhavissati, pīta ti pi na bhavissati, ācariyo ti pi na bhavissati, sippavā ti pi na bhavissati, sīlavā ti pi na bhavissati, paññavā ti pi na bhavissati, kin nu kho mahārāja añña eva kalalassa mātā, aññā abbudassa mātā, aññā pesiyā mātā, aññā ghanassa mātā, aññā khuddakassa mātā, aññā mahantassa mātā, añño sippaṃ sikkhati, añño sikkhito bhavati, añño pāpakammaṃ karoti, aññassa hattha-pādā chijjantī'ti.

Na hi bhante, tvaṃ pana bhante evaṃ vutte kiṃ vadeyyāsī'ti.
Thero āha: ahañ ñeva kho mahārāja daharo ahosiṃ taruṇo mando uttānaseyyako, ahañ ñeva etarahi mahanto, imañ ñeva kāyaṃ nissāya sabbe te ekasaṃgahītā'ti.
(Milindapañha, 2.Chapter, 1. Question)

Fifth Lesson

Training Sentence

(Continuing from last lesson. This is an excerpt form the second chapter of the Milindapañha, see above chapter 4.)

Opammaṃ karohī'ti. - Yathā mahārāja kocid eva
A similie make! As if, Great king somebody even
puriso padīpaṃ padīpeyya, kiṃ so sabbarattiṃ
a man a lamp would get to shine, (what) that all night
dīpeyyā'ti. Āma bhante, sabbarattiṃ dīpeyyā'ti.
could shine? Yes, Sir, all night it could shine."
Kin nu kho mahārāja yā purime yāme
What now Great king, which (it is) in the first watch (of the night)
acci sā majjhime yāme accī'ti.
flame that in the middle watch flame (is)?
Na hi bhante ti. Yā majjhime yāme
"No varily, Sir." – "What in the middle watch
acci sā pacchime yāme accī'ti.
(is that) flame that in the last watch flame is?"
Na hi bhante ti. Kin nu kho mahārāja añño
No, varily, Sir. What now, Great king, another
so ahosi purime yāme padīpo, añño
this was in the first watch light, another
majjhime yāme padīpo, añño pacchime
in the middle watch a light, another in the last
yāme padīpo ti? Na hi bhante, taṃ yeva nissāya
watch a light?" „No, varily, Sir, that even based on

sabbarattiṃ padīpito'ti. Evaṃ eva kho mahārāja
all night it shone. Thus even now great king
dhammasantati sandahati, añño uppajjati
the thing-continuity continues, another appears,
añño nirujjhati, apubbaṃ acarimaṃ viya
another ceases, not-before not-after similar
sandahati, tena na ca so na ca añño
it continues, therefore ‚not the one and not another'
pacchimaviññāṇasaṃgahaṃ gacchatī'ti.
to the last moment of consciousness goes."
Bhiyyo opammaṃ karohī'ti. Yathā mahārāja kīraṃ
More a simile make!" „As the great king milk
duyhamānaṃ kālantarena dadhi parivatteyya
freshly milked after some time (into) curd may turn around,
dadhito navanītaṃ, navanītato ghataṃ
from the curd butter, from the butter ghee
parivatteyya yo nu kho mahārāja evaṃ vadeyya
may turn around, who now, great king, thus may speak
yaṃ yeva kīraṃ, taṃ yeva dadhi, taṃ yeva navanītaṃ
what even milk, that even curd, that even butter,
taṃ yeva ghatan, ti sammā nu kho mahārāja
that even ghee, so right now great king
vadamāno vadeyyā ti? Na hi bhante, taṃ yeva
speaking he would speak? No varily Sir, but on that even
nissāya sambhūtan'ti. Evaṃ eva kho mahārāja
based (it) has become". „So even (is it) now, great king
dhammasantati sandahati, añño uppajjati,
the continuity of things proceeds, another appears
añño nirujjhati, apubbaṃ acarimaṃ viya

another ceases, not before not after similar
sandahati tena na ca so na ca añño
it proceeds, therefore not the same nor another
pacchimaviññāṇasaṃgahaṃ gacchatī'ti.
to the last consciousness moment goes".

Remarks

kocid: through attaching a **-ci** onto the interrogative (questioning) pronoun one creates the indefinite pronoun **koci** = somebody, **kiñci** = something.
In Pāli all words end in a vowel or in the Niggahītaṃ. The closing consonants of the older languages *ved*ic (or classical *sanskrit)* have disappeared. Sometimes, however, these closing consonant forms can appear in front of a following word which starts with a vowel, for example **kocid eva** = somebody (eva remains untranslated), **etad avoca** = this he said.
padīpeyya √ dīp = to shine, from a lamp.

When adding **–aya-** to the stem of a verb we create the **causative**, this verb form expresses that something is being caused to be done/happen.

Very often this "**aya**" is being shortened to "**e**" in the same way as we can find many verbs which have originally an "**ava**-" prefix which they shorten into an "**o**" for instance in **hoti** < bhavati. The prefix **pa-** denotes an "advance" or "out of" like in many English words (be-have, beget,

belittle) it can simply express a strengthening in meaning. So, where is the causative in **padīpeti?** In **dīpayati** or **dīpeti** the causative expresses the meaning of „Making/Causing something that it shines, shine onto, emit light" and **padīpeti** therefore means "to kindle, let something burn"; **padīpeyya** = he, she, it wants/could make it burn; **padīpita** *ppp* = kindled, burning.
dadhito and **navanītato** are rare forms of the *Ablative case*
taṃ yeva is another way of writing **tañ ñeva** (see comments in lesson four)

Translation

" 'Give me an illustration.' 'Suppose a man, O king, were to light a lamp, would it burn the night through?' Yes, it might do so.' 'Now, is it the same flame that burns in the first watch of the night, Sir, and in the second?' 'No.' 'Or the same that burns in the second watch and in the third?' 'No.' 'Then is there one lamp in the first watch, and another in the second, and another in the third?' 'No. The light comes from the same lamp all the night through.' 'Just so, O king, is the continuity of a person or thing maintained. One comes into being, another passes away; and the rebirth is, as it were, simultaneous. Thus neither as the same nor as another does a man go on to the last phase of his self-consciousness.''Give me a further illustration.' 'It is like milk, which when once taken from the cow, turns, after a lapse of time, first to curds, and then from curds to butter, and then from butter to ghee. Now would it be right to say that the milk was the same thing as the curds, or the butter, or the ghee?"Certainly not; but they are produced out of it."Just so, O king, is the continuity of a person or thing maintained. One comes into being, another passes away; and the rebirth is, as it were, simultaneous. Thus neither as the same nor as another does a man go on to the last phase of his self-consciousness.'

Vocabulary

sandahati √ dhā = set together, connect, behave like, appear as if	
nirujjhati √ rudh = to go under, to be destroyed, to cease	
purisa *m* = a man, a person	**padīpa** *m* = lamp
parivattati √ vatt = turn around	**yāma** *m* = nightly watch
viññāṇa *neut* = consciousness	**acci** *f* = flame
navanīta *neut* = fresh butter	**khīra** *neut* = milk
saṃgaha *m* = summary	**ghata** *neut* = ghee
santati *f* = continuity	**dadhi** *neut* = curd
antara neut = the inner	**āma** = yes
kālantara *neut* = timeframe, span of time	**kāla** *m* = time
yathā = as, as soon as	**purima** = first, former, foremost

viya is the same as **iva** = as, as if, similar	**majjhima** = middle
tena (*Instr* from **taṃ**) = through this, therefore, thereby	**pacchima** = last
sambhūta *ppp* von √ **bhū + sam** = brought into existance, appeared	
a-pubba -a-carima = not the former (before), not the later (after)	

Conjugation Present indicative of √ **as** = to be (irregular verb)

	singular		*plural*	
1. person	asmi, amhi	= I am	asma, amha	= we are
2. person	asi	= you are	attha	= you are
3. person	atthi	= he, she, it is	santi	= they are

Participles

The „participle present medii" sometimes has active at other times passive meaning and is created by adding **-māna** to the (present tense) stem of any verb.
For instance:

duyhati (*pass.*) = to be milked;
=> **duyha<u>māna</u>** = being milked, i.e. (milk) which has just been milked;

vadati √ vad = say, talk;
=> **vada<u>māna</u>** = talking; one who talks.

The participle perfect passive (abbreviated as ***ppp***) is created by adding the suffix **-ta** or sometimes **-na** to the root of a verb; **-ta** is quite often added with an –i- as a binding vowel.
<u>Examples</u>.: **padīpita** = kindled; **danta** = tamed; **kata** = done (the latter derived from the root **√ kar** = to make. Here the **-r** of the root has been eliminated during the formation of the past participle.)
gata = gone (from **√ gam** = to go)

Reading exercise

Opammaṃ karohī'ti.
Yathā mahārāja kocid eva puriso padīpaṃ padīpeyya, kiṃ so sabbarattiṃ dīpeyyā'ti. Āma bhante, sabbarattiṃ dīpeyyā'ti.
Kin nu kho mahārāja yā purime yāme acci sā majjhime yāme accī'ti.
Na hi bhante ti. Yā majjhime yāme acci sā pacchime yāme accī'ti.
Na hi bhante ti. Kin nu kho mahārāja añño so ahosi purime yāme padīpo, añño majjhime yāme padīpo, añño pacchime yāme padīpo ti.

Na hi bhante, taṃ yeva nissāya sabbarattiṃ padīpito ti.
Evaṃ eva kho mahārāja dhammasantati sandahati, añño uppajjati añño nirujjhati, apubbaṃ acarimaṃ viya sandahati, tena na ca so na ca añño pacchimaviññāṇasaṃgahaṃ gacchatī'ti.
Bhiyyo opammaṃ karohī'ti.
Yathā mahārāja khīraṃ duyhamānaṃ kālantarena dadhi parivatteyya, dadhito navanītaṃ, navanītato ghataṃ parivatteyya, yo nu kho mahārāja evaṃ vadeyya: yaṃ yeva khīraṃ taṃ yeva dadhi, taṃ yeva navanītaṃ, taṃ yeva ghatan ti sammā nu kho mahārāja vadamāno vadeyyā ti. ---
Evaṃ eva kho mahārāja dhammasantati sandahati, añño uppajjati añño nirujjhati, apubbaṃ acarimaṃ viya sandahati, tena na ca so na ca añño pacchimaviññāṇasaṃgahaṃ gacchatī'ti.

Sixth Lesson

Training sentences

from the Dīgha Nikāya, Mahāparinibbānasutta:

Assosi kho Ambapāligaṇikā bhagavā kira
She heard, Ambapālī, the courtesan: "The Blessed One, as they say,
Vesāliyaṃ anuppatto Vesāliyaṃ viharati mayhaṃ ambavane ti.
in Vesāli has arrived, in Vesāli dwells, in my mango-forest".
Satta vo bhikkhave aparihāniye dhamme desessāmi
Seven you monks beneficial things I will teach.
taṃ suṇātha sādhukaṃ manasikarotha bhāsissāmī'ti.
This you hear, put well to your mind, I will speak.
Evaṃ bhante ti. Kho te bhikkhū bhagavato paccassosuṃ
So, Sir! Now the monks to the Blessed One agreed
Etha tumhe bhikkhave samantā Vesāliṃ yathāmittaṃ
Go you monks around Vesālī as far as there are friend
yathāsandiṭṭhaṃ yathāsambhattaṃ vassaṃ upetha
as far as there are acquaintances, donors (and) the rainy-season you enter,
ahaṃ pana idh' eva Beluvagāmake vassaṃ upagacchāmī'ti.
I but here just in the Beluva-market-town the rainy-season enter.
Gaccha tvaṃ Ānanda yāvatikā bhikkhū Rājagahaṃ upanissāya

Go you Ānanda, as many monks Rājagaha-based-on
viharanti te sabbe upaṭṭhānasālāyaṃ sannipātehī'ti.
dwell, they all to the assembly-hall make-come-together".
Āyāṃ' Ānanda yena Koṭigāmo ten' upasaṇkamissāmā'ti.
We go, Ānanda, where the Koṭi-village (is) there we will walk to.
Evaṃ bhante ti āyasmā Ānando bhagavato paccassosi.
So, Sir, the venerable Ānanda to the Blessed One agreed.
Gaṇhāhi Ānanda nisīdanaṃ, yena Cāpālaṃ cetiyaṃ
Grab Ānanda the sitting-rug, where the Cāpāla stupa (is),
ten' upasaṇkamissāma divāvihārāyā'ti.
there we will walk to, for dwelling the day.
Evaṃ bhante ti kho āyasmā Ānanda bhagavato

„So, Sir" thus answered the venerable Ānanda to the Blessed One,
paṭissutvā nisīdanaṃ ādāya bhagavantaṃ
having agreed, having taken the sitting rug, the Blessed One
piṭṭhitopiṭṭhito anubandhi. Atha kho bhagavā bhikkhū
behind-behind he followed. Then now the Blessed One the monks
āmantesi: Handa dāni bhikkhave āmantayāmi vo:
addressed: Well now, o monks, I address you:
vayadhammā saṅkhārā appamādena sampādethā'ti.
The formations are subject to go away, excert relentlessly !
Ayaṃ tathāgatassa pacchimā vācā.
These (were) the Tathagatha's final words.

Remarks

assosi, anubandhi: In case of an aorist a verb very often shows an initial a-prefix in front of its stem. The most common aorist forms are the **i- aorist** and the **s- aorist**. For example: **anubandhi** = he follow*ed* (verb **anubandhati** √ **bandh** = to bind + prefix **anu-** = after/following) **assosi** = he, she listen*ed*, **assosuṃ** = they listen*ed* (√ su, *sanskrit* sru, therefore a double s following the prefix a. The √ in this case is modified to "so".)
√ **su** + prefix **paṭi** = to listen up, to agree;
The rules of sandhi turn **paṭi-assosi** into the modified form **paccassosi** = he agreed, also **paccassosuṃ** = they agreed.
āmantesi = he addresses (√ **mant** = to talk, to consult with + prefix -**ā**= towards, to).
anuppatta *ppp* of √ **āp** + prefix -**pa**- = to attain + prefix **anu**- = towards, following along: arrived at, came to (double -p, because of *sanskrit* **anupra**-) This Pāli verb form would look in Sanskrit thus: **anu-pa-āpta**.
bhikkhave, *voc pl* , is a so-called "Magadhism", a particular variant of the regular declension pattern due to a dialect of Pāli spoken in Māgadha (a kingdom at the time of the Buddha). The declension pattern in Pāli should rather be *neut pl* **bhikkhavo**.
aparihāniye: **parihāni** *f* = the demise/decay, **parihāniya** = leading to decay/demise, **a-parihāniya** = literally: not leading towards decay; it has a positive connotation and could therefore be translated as: conducive, beneficial.
desessāmi is the futur form of **deseti** (*caus*) √ **dis** = to show, to instruct, to teach.

manasikaroti: **karoti** is *pres* of √ **kar** = to make + **mana** neut = the mind, the thinking, the mental base; therefore = thinking about, think of, to mentally digest something. In its meditative meaning it figuratively means to attend to something to direct ones attention. **yathāmittaṃ** is an adverb, build from **yathā** = as far as, like **mitta** *m* = friend; therefore: as far as there are friends, similar **yathā-sandiṭṭhaṃ** = as far as there are acquaintants and **yathāsambhatthaṃ** = as far as there are hosts.

Translation

She heard, Ambapālī, the courtesan: "The Blessed One, as they say, in Vesāli has arrived, in Vesāli dwells, in my mango-forest". Seven you monks beneficial things I will teach. This you hear, put well to your mind, I will speak. So, Sir! Now the monks to the Blessed One agreed Go you monks around Vesālī as far as there are friend as far as there are acquaintances, donors (and) the rainy-season you enter, I but here just in the Beluva-market-town the rainy-season enter.
Go you Ānanda, as many monks Rājagaha based on dwell, they all to the assembly-hall make come together". We go, Ānanda, where the Koṭi-village (is) there we will walk to. So, Sir, the venerable Ānanda to the Blessed One agreed. Grab Ānanda the sitting-rug, where the Cāpāla stupa (is), there we will walk to, for dwelling the day. „So, Sir" thus answered the venerable Ānanda to the Blessed One, having agreed, having taken the sitting rug, the

Blessed One behind-behind he followed. Then now the Blessed One the monks addressed: Well now, o monks, I address you: The formations are subject to go away, excert relentlessly! These (were) the Tathagatha's final words.

Vocabulary

viharati √ har = to hold, bring + prefix **vi** = apart : to dwell, to rest	
upanissāya = close by, based (on), with help (of)	
vihāra *m* = The dwelling, living, monastery	
āyāti √ yā = to go + prefix **ā-** = to go close to, to come	
upaṭṭhāna neut = showing respect, service + **sāla** *f* = hall = town hall / meeting place.	
eti √ i (modified into **e**) = to go, go to, come	
upeti √ i + upa = to go up to, to reach, (rainy season retreat) to observe	
sampadeti *caus* v. **√ pad** = to fall + sam = together; = 1 to produce, 2 strife for, endeavour	
sannipatati √ pat = fall, + sam + ni = to assemble, meet together, sannipāteti *Caus* = to bring together, to call to assembly	
kira = they say, as they say, it was said	
upagacchati √ gam = same as upeti	**gaṇhati √ pat** = to grab, to take
vaya *m* = demise, decay	**vācā** *f* = word, speech
sambhatta *m* = host,	**ganikā** *f* = courtesan

~friend	
amba *m* = mango	**bhatta** neut = meal, nourishment
bhāsati √ **bhās** = to say, talk	**vayadhamma** = perishing, law of impermanence
nisīdana neut = seat	**saṅkhāra** *m* = formation, activity, fabrication
gāma *m* = village, -ka = small village	**cetiya** neut = tome, stupa, holy place
pamāda *m* = negligence	**appamāda** *m* = earnestness
yāvatika = as big/great as	**āyasmat** = venerable
vana neut = forest, woods	**vassa** neut = rain season
mitta *m* = friend	**satta** = seven
piṭṭhito = back-, behind-	**sādhukaṃ** = good, right
yathā = as	**diṭṭha** *ppp* **√ dis** = to see, seen, viewed, understood
dāni = now	**sandiṭṭha** = seen, having known (m friend)
samantā = around	**divā** = during the day
yena (*I* from **yaṃ**) = where?	**tena** (*I* from **taṃ**) = there, thence
handa = well then!, well!, please!	

Declension of personal pronouns

		Singular		
N	**ahaṃ**	= I	**tvaṃ**	= you
G+D	**mama, mayhaṃ, me**	= my, mine, for me	**tava, tuyhaṃ, te**	= yours, for you
A	**maṃ, mamaṃ**	= to me	**tvaṃ, tavaṃ**	= to you
I	**mayā, me**	= through me	**tvayā, te**	= through you
Ab	**mayā**	= from me	**tvayā**	= from you
L	**mayi**	= in/near me	**tvayi**	= in/near you
		Plural		
N	**mayaṃ, amhe**	= we	**tumhe**	= you
G+D	**amhākaṃ, amhe, no**	= our	**tumhākaṃ, tumhe, vo**	= yours
A	**amhākaṃ, amhe, no**	= us	**tumhākaṃ, tumhe, vo**	= you
I+Ab	**amhehi**	= through us	**tumhehi**	= through you
L	**amhesu**	= at our	**tumhesu**	= at your

IMPORTANT - The **Genitiv** of the personal pronoun replaces the **possessive pronoun**:

mama, mayhaṃ, me = my
tava, tuyhaṃ, te = your
amhakaṃ, no = our
tumhakaṃ, vo = your

The verb √ su = to listen, adds in the present tense and in the imperative forms as well as in the optative the particle "**-no**" or "**-nā**" to the *root;* in the 3. person *plural* however only a "**ṇa**" will occur:

	singular	*plural*
1. person	suṇomi, suṇāmi	suṇoma, suṇāma
2. person	suṇosi, suṇāsi	suṇotha, suṇātha
3. person	suṇoti, suṇāti	suṇanti

*The **absolutivum** also called **gerund***

...are created by adding the suffix **-tvā** or **-ya** to the root of a verb, sometimes adding a intermediate copula letter like **-i-**.

The meaning of the absolutivum/gerund: an activity or occurance which happened before the time of the activity of the main sentence.

English: "after (having done something)".
Examples: **paṭisutvā** = after (he) had agreed, after having agreed;
ādāya (from√ dā = to give + prefix ā- = towards: to take) = after having taken up.

This grammatical form is also known as adverbial participle.

Reading exercise

Assosi kho Ambapālīgaṇikā bhagavā kira Vesāliyaṃ anupatto Vesāliyaṃ viharati mayhaṃ ambavane ti. Satta vo bhikkhave aparihāniye dhamme desessāmi taṃ suṇātha sādhukaṃ manasikarotha bhāsissāmī'ti. Evaṃ bhante ti kho te bhikkhū bhagavato paccassosuṃ. Etha tumhe bhikkhave samantā Vesāliṃ yathāmittaṃ yathāsandiṭṭhaṃ yathāsambhattaṃ vassaṃ upetha, ahaṃ pana idh' eva Beluvagāmake vassaṃ upagacchāmī'ti. Gaccha tvaṃ Ānanda yāvatikā bhikkhū Rājagahaṃ upanissāya viharanti te sabbe upaṭṭhānasālāyaṃ sannipātehī'ti. Āyaṃ' Ānanda yena Koṭigāmo ten' upasaṇkamissāmā'ti. Evaṃ bhante ti āyasmā Ānando bhagavato paccassosi. Gaṇhāhi Ānanda nisīdanaṃ, yena Cāpālaṃ cetiyaṃ ten' upasaṇkamissāma divāvihārāyā'ti.

Evaṃ bhante ti kho āyasmā Ānando bhagavato paṭissutvā nisīdanaṃ ādāya bhagavantaṃ piṭṭhito piṭṭhito anubandhi.
Atha kho bhagavā bhikkhū āmantesi:
Handa dāni bhikkhave āmantayāmi vo:
vayadhammā saṅkhārā, appamādena sampādethā'ti.
Ayaṃ tathāgatassa pacchimā vācā.

Seventh Lesson

Training sentences

from the Mahāparinibbānasutta:

Bhagavā arahaṃ sammā-sambuddho pañca nīvaraṇe
The Blessed One, Worthy One, Fully-Awakened One, the five hindrances
pahāya cetaso upakkilese paññāya
having given up, the mind's defilements having known,
dubbalīkaraṇe catusu satipaṭṭhānesu
the weakening, with regard to the four pillars of memory,
supatiṭṭhitacitte satta bojjhaṅge
with well founded mind the seven members-of-awakening
yathābhūtaṃ bhāvetvā anuttaraṃ sammā-
as-they-have-become having developed to the highest full-
sambodhiṃ abhisambuddho. Imasmiṃ kho
Awakening to the highest Enlightenment. In this now
Subhadda dhammavinaye ariyo aṭṭhaṅgiko maggo
Subhadda teaching and guidance the eightfold path
upalabbhati, idh' eva Subhadda samaṇo, idha dutiyo
is attained, just here Subhadda one ascetic (is), here a second
samaṇo, idha tatiyo samaṇo, idha catuttho samaṇo,
ascetic, here a third ascetic, here a fourth ascetic,
suññā parappavādā samaṇehi aññe, ime ca
empty (are) the school of other ascetics, these and
Subhadda bhikkhū sammā vihareyyuṃ, asuñño

Subhadda monks right live, not empty
loko arahantehi assa. Ekūnatiṃso vayasā Subhadda
this world of arahants would be. Twenty-nine years, Subhadda
yaṃ pabbajiṃ kiṃkusalānuesī.
(is it) that I have renounced searching what-is-beneficial.
Vassāni paññāsasamādhikāni yato ahaṃ pabbajito
Rainy seasons fifty beyond that I renounced
Subhadda, ñāyassa dhammassa padesavattī
Subhadda, of the correct truthful path walking.
Ito bahiddhā samaṇo pi n'atthi.
From here outside an ascetic too is not.

Atha kho bhagavā bhikkhū āmantesi:
Then now the Blessed One addressed the monks:
Siyā kho pana bhikkhave ekabhikkhussa pi kaṅkhā
It may be, o monks, that one-monk's too is doubt
vā vimati vā buddhe vā dhamme vā
or uncertainty with regard to the Buddha or Dhamma
saṅghe vā magge vā paṭipadāya vā
or Sangha or the path or the practice.
pucchatha bhikkhave 'ti.
asked, o monks!

Remarks

nīvaraṇe = **nīvaraṇāni** (neut pl).
paññāya is the gerund of **pajānāti** √ ñā + prefix pa = to

recognize, understand, know; the exact same form could also be a *G*, *D*, or *I* of the noun **paññā** *f* = wisdom, knowing. (*see 2nd lesson*).

dubbalīkaraṇe is composed of: The prefix **du-** = bad, difficult; **bala** = power, force; as in *adj* **balin** = powerful, strong; **karaṇe**: √ kar = to make, do; => therefore un-strong-making, i.e. weakening.

catusu satipaṭṭhānesu: the *L* is used here like an instrumental case.

supatiṭṭhitacitte is *locativus absolutus*, prefix **su-** = good

bojjhaṅga *m pl* is composed of **bodhi** *f* = Awakening, Enlightenment + **aṅga** neut = Member (of the body), part; according to the rules of sandhi (in order to sound well for a native speaker of Pāli) "**bodhiaṅga"** becomes **bodhyaṅga** and eventually **bojjhaṅga.**

bhāveti *caus* of **bhavati** = to make something happen, to create, to develop,to awaken, to cultivate something.

abhisambuddho: prefix **abhi**- = expressing an intensification to the highest, **sam-** = usually 'together', here however in the sense of complete, fully; **buddho** *ppp* of the verb **bujjhati** √ budh = to wake up, to understand

upalabbhati is *pass* of **upalabhati** √ labh = to attain + prefix **upa**- = to here, to, on, up, near = to exist, to find to exist.

kiṃkusalānuesi a composita from **kiṃ** = what?, **kusala** = beneficial, wholesome, good, **anu-esi** √ i = to go + **anu** = after; ==> therfore to follow after, search; **esi** is the aorist of **eti**; therefore: "he searched, what is beneficial" The final **-i** was lengthened due to the verse metrics to an **ī.**

paññāsasamādhikāni consists of **paññāsa** = fifty, **samā** *f* = years, **adhika** = going beyond.

padesa-vattī: **padesa** *m* = area, region, place; + **vattin** from **vattati** √ vatt = to turn, to go, to wander, therefore: someone who walks for a certain distance (+ *L*)

Translation

"And the Blessed One too, Lord, being at present the Arahant, the Fully Enlightened One, has abandoned the five hindrances, the mental defilements that weaken wisdom; has well established his mind in the four foundations of mindfulness; has duly cultivated the seven factors of enlightenment, and is fully enlightened in unsurpassed, supreme Enlightenment."

Now in this Dhamma and Discipline, Subhadda, is found the Noble Eightfold Path; and in it alone are also found true ascetics of the first, second, third, and fourth degrees of saintliness. Devoid of true ascetics are the systems of other teachers. But if, Subhadda, the bhikkhus live righteously, the world will not be destitute of arahats.

"In age but twenty-nine was I, Subhadda,
When I renounced the world to seek the Good;
Fifty-one years have passed since then, Subhadda,
And in all that time a wanderer have I been

In the domain of virtue and of truth,
And except therein, there is no saint (of the first degree).

Then the Blessed One addressed the bhikkhus, saying: "It may be, bhikkhus, that one of you is in doubt or perplexity as to the Buddha, the Dhamma, or the Sangha, the path or the practice. Then question, bhikkhus!

Vocabulary

kaṅkhā *f* = doubt	**yato** = where, when, as
vimati *f* = uncertainty	**ariya** *adj* = noble
bahiddhā = outside, outer	**nīvaraṇa** neut = hindrance
aṭṭhaṅgika = eightfold	**ceta** neut = mind, intention, will
asuñña = not empty	**kusala** = wholesome, benficial, good.
upakkilesa *m* = defilement	**aṅga** neut = member, part of the body
vinaya *m* = rules of the order, discipline, training.	**citta** neut = thinking, heart, mind
para = far, foreign, opposing	**samā** *f* = year
vaya neut (*ved* váyas) = age of life	**vadati** √ vad = to say, to talk
uttara = higher	**an-uttara** = nothing higher, the highest

yaṃ = that, as	**vattin** *m* = wanderer
ito = from here	**upaṭṭhāna** neut = setting up
bodhi *f* = awakening, enlightenment	

sati *f* = mindfulness, memory, witnessing, carefulness
pajahāti √ hā + pa = let, let go, eave, gerundivum being **pahāya**
patiṭṭhāti √ ṭhā = to stand + pa = to stand tight, to be protected; *ppp* **patiṭṭhita** + prefix **su-** = well = well protected, very secure
parappavāda *m* = debate with another sectarian/school of thought
ñāya *m* = method, system, right path, (logic)
padesa *m* = area, region, place, land
suñña = empty, waste
suññatā *f* = emptiness
yathābhūtaṃ = "as it is", according to truth, lit.: as it has become.

Numerals

eka	1	ekādasa	11	ekavīsa	21
dvi	2	dvādasa	12	bāvīsati	22
te, ti	3	terasa	13	tevīsa	23
catu	4	cuddasa	14	ekūnatiṃsa	29

pañca	5	pañcadasa, pannarasa	15	tiṃsa, tiṃsati	30
cha	6	soḷasa	16	ekatiṃsa	31
satta	7	sattarasa	17	paññāsa, paṇṇāsā	50
aṭṭha	8	aṭṭhārasa	18	sata	100
nava	9	ekūnavīsa	19	satassa	1000
dasa	10	vīsaṃ, vīsati	20	lakkhaṃ	100 000

The remaining numerals occur very seldom.

Cardinal numbers

paṭhama = first,
dutiya = second, **tatiya** = third, **catuttha** = fourth, **pañcama** = fifth
These are the most frequent cardinal numbers.

Declension of basic numerals

Eka = one and **sabba** = all, both follow in their *singular* form the nouns of the -a declension; in their *pl* forms they are declined like **so** = he/this.
Dvi, ti and **catu** follow the declination pattern of nouns ending in -i or -u *pl*. There are however a few irregular forms which will be found in most Pali dictionaries. Most of the other numerals are declined according to nouns of

the -a declension (plural) with some irregular forms among them.

The s-Declension:

Nouns which end in **-as** (see 3rd Lesson) in their stem very often are declined as if their stem would just end in -a, they therefore follow the -a declension.
Besides this major pattern some older forms however remain and tell the story of the originally separate -as declension.
Examples.: **manas** neut = mind, mental sense-base.
vacas neut = speech, saying

	Singular	
N	mano	Vaco
G+D	manaso	Vacaso
A	mano	Vaco
I	manasā	Vacasā
Ab	manasā	Vacasā
L	manasi	Vacasi
V	mana	Vaca

Conjugation of Aorist forms

pabbaji from **pabbajati √ baj** = to go, to pace + prefix. **pa** = for-; equals "to go forth", to go from home into homelessness.
anu-esi see remark above

Below the irregular Optativ *of* ***atthi √ as*** *= to be*

	singular	*Plural*
1. person	assaṃ = I may	assāma = we may
2. person	assa = you may	assatha = you may
3. person	assa, siyā = he, she, it may	assu, siyuṃ = they may

Reading exercise

Bhagavā arahaṃ sammāsambuddho pañca nīvaraṇe pahāya cetaso upakkilese paññāya dubbalīkaraṇe catusu satipaṭṭhānesu supatiṭṭhitacitte satta bojjhaṅge yathābhūtaṃ bhāvetvā anuttaraṃ sammāsambodhiṃ abhisambuddho. Imasmiṃ kho Subhadda dhammavinaye ariyo aṭṭhaṅgiko maggo upalabbhati, idh' eva Subhadda samaṇo, idha dutiyo samaṇo, idha tatiyo samaṇo, idha catuttho samaṇo, suññā parappavādā samaṇehi aññe, ime ca Subhadda bhikkhū sammā vihareyyuṃ, assuñño loko arahantehi assa.

Ekūnatiṃso vayasā Subhadda
yaṃ pabbajiṃ kiṃkusalānuesī.
Vassāni paññāsasamādhikāni
yato ahaṃ pabbajito Subhadda,
ñāyassa dhammassa padesavattī.
Ito bahiddhā samaṇo pi nātthi.

Atha kho bhagavā bhikkhū amantesi:
Siyā kho pana bhikkhave ekabhikkhussa pi kaṅkhā vā vimati vā buddhe vā dhamme vā saṅghe vā magge vā paṭipadāya vā pucchatha bhikkhave'ti.

Eigth Lesson

Training sentences

from the Mahāparinibbānasutta:

Supaṭipanno bhagavato sāvakasaṅgho
Well faring is the Blessed One's Order of Disciples
ujupaṭipanno bhagavato sāvakasaṅgho
righteously,
ñāyapaṭipanno bhagavato sāvakasaṅgho
wisely,
sāmīcipaṭipanno bhagavato sāvakasaṅgho
dutifully faring is the Blessed One's Order of Disciples
Yadidaṃ cattāri purisayugāni aṭṭha purisapuggalā
That is to say, the four pairs of men, the eight classes of persons,
esa bhagavato sāvakasaṅgho āhuṇeyyo
dThe Blessed One's Order of Disciples is worthy of honor
pāhuṇeyyo dakkhiṇeyyo añjalikaraṇīyo
of hospitality, of offerings, of veneration
anuttaraṃ puññakhettaṃ lokassā'ti.
the supreme field for meritorious deeds in the world.

Kathaṃ mayaṃ bhante mātugāme paṭipajjāmā'ti.
How, Lord, should we conduct ourselves towards women?"
Adassanaṃ Ānanda 'ti.
"Do not see them, Ananda."

Dassane bhagavā sati kathaṃ paṭipajjitabban 'ti.
"But, Lord, if we do see them?"
Anālāpo Ānanda 'ti.
"Do not speak, Ananda."
Ālapantena pana bhante kathaṃ paṭipajjitabban 'ti.
"But, Lord, if they should speak to us?"
Sati Ānanda upaṭṭhāpetabbā 'ti.
"Then, Ananda, you should establish mindfulness."

From the **Saṃyuttanikāya** (XXII,94):

Nāhaṃ bhikkhave lokena vivadāmi, loko ca mayā vivadati.
Not I, (you) monks, quarrel with the world; the world quarrels with me.
Na bhikkhave dhammavādī kenaci
Not, o monks, does a speaker-of-the-truth with anyone
lokasmiṃ vivadati. Yaṃ bhikkhave natthi sammataṃ
in the world quarrel. What, o monks, "it is not" explained
loke paṇḍitānaṃ, ahaṃ pi taṃ natthī'ti vadāmi.
in the world of the wise ones, I too that "it is not" say.
Yaṃ bhikkhave atthi sammataṃ loke paṇḍitānaṃ,
What, o monks, "it is" explained in the world of the wise ones,
ahaṃ pi taṃ atthī'ti vadāmi.
I too that "it is" say.

Remarks

sāmīcipaṭipanno: **sāmīci** equals **sammā** = right, correct
āhuṇeyyo pāhuṇeyyo = **ā-hav-aṇīya, pa-ā-hav-aṇīya**, **√ hu** = sacrifice intensified to **hav**; from the **-ava-** constructed in this way we would have expected a contraction into **-o-**, instead we find the root **√ hu** again; **-eyyo** instead of **-īyo** possibly because it follows the regularly constructed verbal adjective (see next)
dakkhiṇeyyo; with a prefix of **ā-** and **pa-ā-** which intensify the meaning "to sacrifice, give" i.e. worthy of worship and gifts.
dassane sati: *Locativus absolutus.*; **sati** is a *Locative form* of the *present participle* **sant** from **√ as** = being.
ālapante is *I* instrumental for *L* and stands here for the *Locativus absolutus.*

Translation

Well faring is the Blessed One's Order of Disciples, righteously, wisely, and dutifully: that is to say, the four pairs of men, the eight classes of persons. The Blessed One's Order of Disciples is worthy of honor, of hospitality, of offerings, of veneration — the supreme field for meritorious deeds in the world.'. The world quarrels with me."

"How, Lord, should we conduct ourselves towards women?""Do not see them, Ananda.""But, Lord, if we do see them?""Do not speak, Ananda.""But, Lord, if they should speak to us?""Then, Ananda, you should establish mindfulness."

"Not do I, o monks, quarrel with the world, but the world quarrels with me. Who talks right and truthful such a one does not quarrel with the world. Of what the wise ones say "it is not" of that I too say: "it is not". Of what the wise ones say that "it is" of that I too say: "it is not"

Vocabulary

ñāya *m* = method, system	**yuga** neut = yoke, pair
puggala *m* = person, individual	**añjali** *m* = bow and clasp hands greeting
mātugāma *m* = women folk, women	**khetta** neut = field
dassana neut = looking	**ālāpa** *m* = chat, talk
ālapati √ lap = talk + ā = talk to	**uju** = straight, upright
paṇḍita *m* = wise man, scholar	**yadidaṃ** = namely
sāvaka *m* = student, pupil, follower	**dhammavādin** = someone who speaks the truth
upaṭṭhāti √ ṭhā = stand + upa = stand up, appear	
upaṭṭhāpeti *caus* = to make that something arises, to pull up	
vivadati √ vad = to talk + vi- = to talk apart, i.e to quarrel	

sammata *ppp* from **sammaññati** √ man = to mean, think + sam = together, to agree

paṭipajjati √ pad + paṭi = 1 to reach, to get to 2 Following a path or method

paṭipanna = *ppp* = ~ having followed a path or method

Conjugation of verbal adjectives (*Potential Participles*)

To express that something, which needs to be done, has to be done, or should/could be done the Pāli language has a suffix which it adds to the root of verbs. This suffix is either **-tabba** or **-anīya** or else **-aṇīya** / **-ya**, sometimes also to the stem (**-tabba** with a binding -i- attached to the present tense stem).
Roots which appear in front of a **-ya** change their roots. They will change their ending **-a** into an **e** and double the **y**.

Examples

ramati √ ram = to be delighted **==>** **ramanīya** = that, which makes one delighted, beautiful
karoti √ kar = to make > **karaṇīya** = that, which has to be made, the duty. Or, someone for whom one has to do something.
pibati √ pā = to drink > **panīya** = something that one has to drink. Drinkable food, i.e. a soup, a drink
dakkhiṇāti from **dakkhiṇā** *f* = sacrifice, oblation, offering (give to brahmins) i.e. to give offerings, to give some kind

of tribute
dakkhiṇeyya = someone, to whom offerings should be given
paṭipajjati √ pad = to go to, to get to, follow (a path, method)
pañipajjitabba = how has to be followed (proceeded), how can be achieved,
upaṭṭhāpeti *caus* of **upaṭṭhāti** = to set up, to keep prepared
upaṭṭhāpetabba = what has to be set up, what has to be kept prepared
añjālikaraṇīya = someone, to whom one has to extand a greeting, i.e. someone worthy of reference, worship, veneration
āhuṇeyya, pāhuṇeyya = irregular verbal adjectives, see above!

Reading exercise

supaṭipanno bhagavato sāvakasaṅgho, ujupaṭipanno bhagavato sāvakasaṅgho, ñāyapaṭipanno bhagavato sāvakasaṅgho, sāmīcipaṭipanno sāvakasaṅgho, yadidaṃ cattāri purisayugāni aṭṭha purisapuggalā, esa bhagavato sāvakasaṅgho, āhuṇeyyo, pāhuṇeyyo, dakkhiṇeyyo, añjālikaraṇīyo anuttaraṃ puññakkhettaṃ lokassā'ti.
Kathaṃ mayaṃ bhante mātugāme paṭipajjāmā 'ti.
Adassanaṃ Ānanda 'ti.
Dassane bhagavā sati kathaṃ paṭipajjitabban'ti. Anālāpo Ānanda 'ti.
Ālapantena pana bhante kathaṃ paṭipajjitabban 'ti.
Sati Ānanda upaṭṭhāpetabbā'ti.

Nāhaṃ bhikkhave, lokena vivadāmi, loko ca mayā vivadati.
Na bhikkhave dhammavādī kenaci lokasmiṃ vivadati.
Yaṃ bhikkhave natthi sammataṃ loke paṇḍitānaṃ, ahaṃ pi taṃ natthī'ti vadāmi.
Yaṃ bhikkhave atthi sammataṃ loke paṇḍitānaṃ, ahaṃ pi taṃ atthī'ti vadāmi.

Ninth Lesson

Training passages

from the *Mahāparinibbānasutta (DN 16)*

Yathā kho pan' Ānanda etarahi bhikkhū aññamaññaṃ
And, Ananda, whereas now the bhikkhus one another
āvusovādena samudācaranti, na vo mam' accayena
as 'friend,' address, not be so after my passing.
evaṃ samudācaritabbaṃ, theratarena Ānanda bhikkhunā
so should be addressed, from the elder, Ānanda, a monk
navakataro bhikkhu nāmena vā gottena vā āvusovādena
a younger monk with name or family or friend - address
vā samudācaritabbo, navakatarena bhikkhunā therataro
is to be addressed; a younger monk an elder
bhikkhu bhante ti vā āyasmā ti vā samudācaritabbo.
monk with 'Sir' or 'Venerable' is to be addressed..

Alaṃ Ānanda mā soci mā paridevi, na nu etaṃ Ānanda
Enough, Ānanda, do not despair. do not be saddened, well is not this Ānanda
mayā paṭigacc' eva akkhātaṃ sabbeh' eva piyehi
from me formerly well explained, from all even loved (things)
manāpehi nānābhāvo vinābhāvo
agreeable (things) a different-becoming a separate-becoming,
aññathābhāvo, taṃ kut' ettha Ānanda labbhā:

a different-becoming, (is) this well here Ānanda, attainable:
yaṃ taṃ jataṃ bhūtaṃ saṅkhataṃ palokadhammaṃ
that that which is born, become, formed, subject to change,
taṃ vata mā palujjīti, n'etaṃ ṭhānaṃ vijjati.
that it varily should not fall apart, not is this case be found.

From the Udāna:
Acchijji vaṭṭaṃ, byāgā nirāsaṃ,
Cut off is the revolving, attained the wishlessness,
visukkhā saritā na sandati, chinnaṃ vaṭṭaṃ
the dry river does not flow any more, the destroyed wheel
na vattati, es' ev' anto dukkhassa.
does not turn, such is the end of suffering (VII, 2)

Bhavavippahānāya kho pan' idaṃ
For the giving-up-of-being but this
brahmacariyaṃ vussati.
brahma-(like)-life is being lived. (III,10)

Remarks

byāgā = vyāgā = vi-ā-gā, aorist of **√ gam** = to go i.e. go away from, get away from; he got away, he is freed.

Translation:
And, Ananda, whereas now the bhikkhus address one another as 'friend,' let it not be so when I am gone. The senior bhikkhus, Ananda, may address the junior ones by

their name, their family name, or as 'friend'; but the junior bhikkhus should address the senior ones as 'venerable sir' or 'your reverence.'

"Enough, Ananda! Do not grieve, do not lament! For have I not taught from the very beginning that with all that is dear and beloved there must be change, separation, and severance? Of that which is born, come into being, compounded, and subject to decay, how can one say: 'May it not come to dissolution!'? There can be no such state of things.

Cut off is the revolving, attained the wishlessness, the dry river does not flow any more, destroyed wheel so that it does not turn, such is the end of suffering.

For the giving up of existance is this pure life being led.

Vocabulary

paridevati √ div = bewail, moan + pari = to lament	**bhāva** *m* = becoming, being, existence
cariya neut = lifestyle, leading life	**Brahma~** = holy, pure ~
bhavati √ bhū = to be, exist *ppp* **bhūta** = become	**vinā** = without, except
kuto = from where, how much less	**saritā** *f* = river

vinābhāva *m* = without-becoming, i.e. separation	**etarahi** = now
ṭhāna neut = place, case, situation	**labbhā** = erreichbar
visukkha = dried up / withered away	**nāma** neut = name
accaya *m* = death, passing away	**alaṃ** = enough
paloka neut = decay, demise	**nirāsa** neut = wishlessness
paṭigacc'eva = formerly, preventive	**aññathā** = other, else
samudācarati √ car = move around, + sam-ud-ā = to talk to	**aññaṃ** = other, also, again
jāyati √ jan = to be born *ppp* **jāta** = born	**aññe** = the other, the rest
aññamaññaṃ = one each other, mutual	**añña** (*Pron*) = other
piya = lovely, agreeable, likeable, loved	**nānā** = different, various
socati √ suc = mourning, to be sorrowful	**āvuso** (voc) = dear friend
manāpa = winning over the mind i.e. lovely, enticing, beautiful	**vāda** *m* = speech, address

akkhāti √ **khyā** = to see **+ ā** = to make visilbe = to make known, proclaim

saṅkharoti √ kar = to make + **sam** = to put together

vippahāna neut = giving up, letting go, becoming free of
vaṭṭati √ vaṭṭ = cyrcling, turn around, to be propper
vaṭṭa neut = circle, cycling, (turning of a wheel)
vattati = to happen, to occur, to advance, to exist
vatteti = live life, (power) to exercise, wield

Comparative of the adjectives

The comperative is created by adding **-tara** to the stem.
Examples:
thera = elder becomes **theratara** = elderer
new = new becomes **navatara** = newer
Superlatives are rare. (very often the prefix **abhi**- or **sam**- is used instead)
Diminuitive forms usually end with **-ka**.
Like **gāma** = village and **gāmaka**= market place

Conjugation of the negative imperative

The **negating imperative** is expressed by using the particle **mā** in conjunction with a verb's aorist form.
Examples.: **mā soci** = do not despair!
mā paridevi = do not cry!

The Passive

The **passiv** is created by using the passive stem which itself is achieved by adding **-ya** or **-iya** or **-īya** onto the root.
Ex.: **√ ñā** = to know => **ñāyati** = to be known.
√ ji = to win => **jīyati** = to be beaten.

If a word root ends in a consonant the **y** is then being assimilated with the preceding consonant.
Example.: **√ luj** = to break, destroy + prefix **pa-** = to break, destroy; **pa-luj-ya** becomes **palujja**, therefore passive as **palujjati** = it is being broken up, destroyed; **mā palujji** = it should not be broken up, should not be destroyed.
√ vid = to find, out of **vid-ya** we get **vijja**, therefore **vijjati** = it is being found (the present tense stem adds an **-n-**: **vindati** = he finds)
√ chid = to cut (off); passive stem **chid-ya** = **chijja**, therefore **chijjati** = it is being cut off; aorist **achijji** = it was cut off (here too a **-n-** is inserted: **chindati** = to cut (off))
The roots **√ vas** and **√ vac** and similar ones change during passive stem construction into **vus** and **vuc** etc.; **√ vas** = to dwell, live; passive: **vus-ya** = **vussa**, also **vussati** = is being lived.
√ vac = to say passive: **vuc-ya** = **vucca**, therefore **vuccati** = it is being said, it is called.
√ vah = to drive, move along; passive**: vuh-ya** = **vuyha**, therefore **vuyhati** = is being driven, taken away, moved forward

The conjugation of passive forms is the same as for a-stems.

Reading exercise

Yathā kho pan' Ānanda etarahi bhikkhū aññamaññaṃ āvusovādena samudācaranti, na vo mam' accayena evaṃ samudācaritabbaṃ, theratarena Ānanda bhikkhunā navakataro bhikkhū nāmena vā gottena vā āvusovādena vā samudācaritabbo, navakatarena bhikkhunā therataro bhikkhu bhante ti vā āyasmā ti vā samudācaritabbo. Alaṃ Ānanda mā soci mā paridevi, na nu etaṃ Ānanda mayā paṭigacc' eva akkhātaṃ sabbeh' eva piyehi manāpehi nānābhāvo vinābhāvo aññathābhāvo, taṃ kut' ettha Ānanda labbha: yaṃ taṃ jataṃ bhūtaṃ saṅkhataṃ palokadhammaṃ, taṃ vata mā palujjīti, n'etaṃ ṭhānaṃ vijjati. (Mahāparinibbānasutta)

Bhavavippahānāya kho pan' idaṃ brahmacariyaṃ vussati. (Udāna III, 10)
Acchijji vaṭṭaṃ, byāgā nirāsaṃ, visukkhā sarita na sandati, chinnaṃ vaṭṭaṃ na vattati, es'ev' anto dukkhassa. (Udāna VII, 2)

Tenth Lesson

Training passage
from the *Dhammacakkapavattanasutta (Saṃ. V, 420)*

Evaṃ me sutaṃ. Ekaṃ samayaṃ Bhagavā Bārāṇasiyaṃ
So from me heard. At one time the Blessed One in Benares
viharati Isipatane miga-dāye. Tatra kho bhagavā
dwelled at Isipatane in the forest of deers. There now the Blessed One
pañcavaggiye bhikkhū āmantesi:
the fiver-group of monks addressed:
dve 'me, bhikkhave antā pabbajitena na sevitabbā.
"Two these monks, ends, by a mendicant should not be practiced:
Katame dve? Yo c'āyaṃ kāmesu kāmasukhallikānuyogo
Which two? That which is devoted to sensual pleasure:
hīno gammo pothujjaniko anariyo anatthasaṃhito
base, vulgar, common, ignoble, unprofitable,
yo c'āyaṃ atta-kilamath'ānuyogo dukkho anariyo
and that which is devoted to self-affliction: painful, ignoble.
an-attha-saṃhito, ete kho bhikkhave ubho ante
unprofitable. these, o monks, both extremes
an-upa-gamma majjhimā paṭipadā tathāgatena
avoiding the middle way by the Tathagata
abhisambuddhā cakkhukaraṇī ñāṇakaraṇī upasamāya
was realized, producing vision, producing knowledge

leads to calm,
abhiññāya sambodhāya nibbānāya saṃvattati.
to direct knowledge, to self-awakening, to cessation.
Katamā ca sā bhikkhave paṭipadā tathāgatena
And what is the, o monks, middle way realized by the Tathagata that
abhisambuddhā cakkhukaraṇī ñāṇakaraṇī upasamāya
producing vision, producing knowledge — leads to calm
abhiññāya sambodhāya nibbānāya saṃvattati?
to direct knowledge, to self-awakening, to cessation?
Ayaṃ eva ariyo aṭṭhaṅgiko maggo, seyyath' īdaṃ:
This verily noble Eightfold Path, namely this:
sammādiṭṭhi sammāsaṇkappo sammāvācā sammākammanto
right view, right resolve, right speech, right action,
sammāājīvo sammāvāyāmo sammāsati sammāsamādhi.
right livelihood, right effort, right remembering, right concentration.
Ayaṃ kho sā bhikkhave majjhimā paṭipadā tathāgatena
This is the middle way by the Tathagata
abhisambuddhā cakkhu-karaṇī ñāṇa-karaṇī upasamāya
realized that vision-producing, knowledge-producing — leads to calm,
abhiññāya sambodhāya nibbānāya saṃvattati.
to direct knowledge, to self-awakening, to cessation.
Idaṃ kho pana bhikkhave dukkhaṃ ariya-saccaṃ:
Now this but, monks, is the noble truth of pain:
jāti pi dukkhā, jarā pi dukkhā, vyādhi pi dukkhā,
Birth is painful, aging is painful, illness is painful, ,
maraṇaṃ pi dukkhā, appiyehi sampayogo dukkho,

death is painful, association with the unbeloved is painful,
piyehi vippayogo dukkho, yaṃ p'icchaṃ na labhati
separation from the loved is painful, not getting what is wanted
taṃ pi dukkhaṃ, saṃkhittena pañc'up'ādāna-kkhandhā
that too is painful, in short, the five-heaps-of-uptaking
pi dukkhā. Idaṃ kho pana bhikkhave dukkhasamudayaṃ
are painful. And this but, monks, is of the origination of pain
ariyasaccaṃ: yā'yaṃ taṇhā ponobbhavikā
the noble truth: the craving that (makes) again-being —
nandi-rāga-saha-gatā tatra-tatr'ābhinandinī
accompanied by passion and delight, relishing now here and now there
seyyath'idaṃ: kāma-taṇhā bhava-taṇhā vi-bhava-taṇhā.
namely: craving for sensual pleasure, for becoming, for non-becoming.
Idaṃ kho pana bhikkhave dukkha-nirodhaṃ ariya-saccaṃ:
"And this but, monks, is the noble truth of the cessation of pain:
yo tassā yeva taṇhāya asesavirāganirodho
that remainderless fading and cessation, renunciation, relinquishment,
cāgo paṭinissaggo mutti anālayo. Idaṃ kho pana bhikkhave
release and letting go of that very craving. And this, monks,
dukkha-nirodha-gāminī paṭipadā ariya-saccaṃ

is the noble truth of the way of practice leading to the cessation of pain:
ayaṃ eva ariyo aṭṭhaṇgiko maggo, seyyath'idaṃ:
this verily Noble Eightfold Path, namely:
sammādiṭṭhi sammāsaṇkappo sammāvācā sammākammanto
— right view, right resolve, right speech, right action,
sammāājīvo sammāvāyāmo sammāsati sammāsamādhi.
right livelihood, right effort, right remembering, right concentration.

Remarks

Bārāṇasiyaṃ Isipatane migadāye: if several locations are given in Pāli, the larger or more important place is given in the beginning, followed by the next smaller one. (Note: Benares = Vārāṇasi)
dve'me: here, one **i** was dropped due to the preceding **e**
cāyaṃ is a shortened form and stand for **ca ayaṃ**, similar **yāyaṃ** from **yā ayaṃ**
seyyath'idaṃ = seyyathā idaṃ; due to the contraction of the vowels **ā** and **i** the **i** was lengthened to **ī**; **seyyathā** is dialect (magadha) for **taṃ - yathā** = like this, "i.e.".

Translation

Thus have I heard. At one time the Blessed One was dwelling at Bārāṇasī in the Deer Park at Isipatana. There the Blessed One addressed the bhikkhus of the group of five thus: "Bhikkhus, these two extremes should not be followed by one gone forth (into the homeless life). What two? That which is this pursuit of sensual happiness in sense pleasures, which is low, vulgar, the way of the ordinary person, ignoble, not connected to the goal; and that which is this pursuit of self-mortification, which is painful, ignoble, not connected to the goal. Bhikkhus, without veering towards either of these two extremes, the One Attuned to Reality has awakened to the middle way, which gives rise to vision, which gives rise to knowledge, which leads to peace, to higher knowledge, to full awakening, to Nibbāna.

"And what, bhikkhus, is that middle way awakened to by the One Attuned to Reality which gives rise to vision, which gives rise to knowledge, which leads to peace, to higher knowledge, to full awakening, to Nibbāna? It is just this Noble Eight-factored Path, that is to say, right view, right resolve, right speech, right action, right livelihood, right effort, right mindfulness, right mental unification. '
"Now this, bhikkhus, for the spiritually ennobled ones, is the true reality which is pain: birth is painful, aging is painful, illness is painful, death is painful; sorrow, lamentation, physical pain, unhappiness and distress are painful; union with what is disliked is painful; separation from what is liked is painful; not to get what one wants is painful; in brief, the five bundles of grasping-fuel are painful.

"Now this, bhikkhus, for the spiritually ennobled ones, is the pain-originating true reality. It is this craving which leads to renewed existence, accompanied by delight and attachment, seeking delight now here now there; that is, craving for sense-pleasures, craving for existence, craving for extermination (of what is not liked).

"Now this, bhikkhus, for the spiritually ennobled ones, is the pain-ceasing true reality. It is the remainderless fading away and cessation of that same craving, the giving up and relinquishing of it, freedom from it, non-reliance on it.

"Now this, bhikkhus, for the spiritually ennobled ones, is the true reality which is the way leading to the cessation of pain. It is this Noble Eight-factored Path, that is to say, right view, right resolve, right speech, right action, right livelihood, right effort, right mindfulness, right mental unification. "

Vocabulary

samādhi *m* = concentration	**upādāna** neut = taking up, hold onto
samudaya *m* = arising	**labhati** √ labh = attain, get
rāga *m* = color, passion	**virāga** *m* = de-coloring, ~free of
attha *m* = meaning, reason, goal, target	**anattha** *m* = worthlessness, not a

	target
nandi *m* = delight	**allika** = attached to, clinging to
cakkhu neut = eye	**dāya** *m* = small forest
abhiññā *f* = higher knowledge	**vagga** *m* = group
nibbāna neut = cessation	**kāma** *m* = sensual lust, greed, sensual object
saṇkappa *m* = intention, attitude	**sukha** neut = happiness
kammanta *m* = doing, deed	**vāyāma** *m* = fight
kilamatha neut = torment	**paṭipadā** *f* = path, right path
ponobbhavika = leading to new being	**upasama** *m* = stilling, peace
sambodhi *f* = complete awakening	**anālaya** *m* = turning away, not-clinging
sesa = remaining	**asesa** = without remainder
katama = which	**vācā** *f* = speech, speaking
diṭṭhi *f* = view, theory, dogma	**ājīva** *m* = way of life
miga *m* = gazelle	**jarā** *f* = aging
vyādhi *f* = disease	**maraṇa** *neut* = dying, death
gamma = village-like, rural, low (gāma)	**anuyoga** = ardous, avid, busy
icchā *f* = wish, a desire	**nirodha** *m* = extinction
ariya = noble	**anariya** = not noble
khandha *m* = group,	**karaṇa** = making, doing

aggregate	
hīna = low, small, inferior	**tatra** = there
paṭinissaga *m* = letting go, giving up, forsaking	**appiya** = not dear
mutti *f* = freedom, release	**cāga** *m* = giving up, renouncing
pi (after a word) = and, also	**pi ... pi** = as well as
sevati √ sev = serve, follow, to be used to, to indulge	**pothujjanika** = mundane
sati *f* = remembrance, memory, witnessing, being careful, mindfulness	
sahagata *ppp* **√ gam + saha** = with- i.e. gone with, joined	
saṃkhittena *Instr.* of *ppp* **√ khip** = throw, + prefix. **sam-** = together.: abbreviated, short	
atta- (in composita) = self-	**abhinandin** = to be enchanted, to like(*f* + ī)
ubho (*Adj pl*) = both	**gāmin** = leading (*f* + ī)

ubho is (except for **dve** = two) the only dual form in Pāli. Declined as:
N ubho, **G+D** ubhinnaṃ, **A** ubho, **I+Ab** ubhohi, ubhehi, **L** ubhesu, **Voc** ubho

Reading exercise

Evaṃ me sutaṃ. Ekaṃ samayaṃ Bhagavā Bārāṇasiyaṃ viharati Isipatane migadāye. Tatra kho bhagavā

pañcavaggiye bhikkhū āmantesi:
Dve'me bhikkhave antā pabbajitena na sevitabbā. Katame dve? Yo cāyaṃ kāmesu kāmasukhallikānuyogo hīno gammo pothujjaniko anariyo anatthasaṃhito, yo cāyaṃ attakilamathānuyogo dukkho anariyo anatthasaṃhito, ete kho bhikkhave ubho ante anupagamma majjhimā paṭipadā tathāgatena abhisambuddhā cakkhu-karaṇī ñāṇakaraṇī upasamāya abhiññāya sambodhāya nibbānāya saṃvatta-ti. Katamā ca sā bhikkhave paṭipadā tathāgatena abhisambuddhā cakkhukaraṇī ñāṇakaraṇī upasamāya abhiññāya sambodhāya nibbānāya saṃvattati.
Ayaṃ eva ariyo aṭṭhaṅgiko maggo seyyath'īdaṃ: sammādiṭṭhi sammāsaṇkappo sammāvācā sammākammanto sammāājīvo sammāvāyāmo sammāsati sammāsamādhi.
Ayaṃ kho sā bhikkhave majjhimā paṭipadā tathāgatena abhisambuddhā cakkhukaraṇī ñāṇakaraṇī upasamāya abhiññāya sambodhāya nibbānāya saṃvattati.
Idaṃ kho pana bhikkhave dukkhaṃ ariyasaccaṃ:
jāti pi dukkhā, jarā pi dukkhā, vyādhi pi dukkhā, maraṇaṃ pi dukkhaṃ appiyehi sampayogo dukkho, piyehi vippayogo dukkho, yaṃ p'icchaṃ na labhati, taṃ pi dukkhaṃ, saṃkhittena pañc' upādānakkhandhā pi dukkhā.
Idaṃ kho pana bhikkhave dukkhasamudayaṃ ariyasaccaṃ:
yāyaṃ taṇhā ponobbhavikā nandirāgasahagatā tatratatrābhinandinī, seyyath'īdaṃ: kāmataṇhā bhavataṇhā vibhavataṇhā.

Idaṃ kho pana bhikkhave dukkhanirodhaṃ ariyasaccaṃ:
yo tassā yeva taṇhāya asesavirāganirodho cāgo
paṭinissaggo mutti anālayo.
Idaṃ kho pana bhikkhave dukkhanirodhagāminī paṭipadā
ariyasaccaṃ ayaṃ eva ariyo aṭṭhaṅgiko maggo,
seyyath'īdaṃ:
sammādiṭṭhi sammāsaṇkappo sammāvācā
sammākammanto sammāājīvo sammāvāyāmo sammāsati
sammāsamādhi.

Index of References

Lesson 1
Dhammapada v. 5 I Cullavagga VII,3,12 (Vinaya Piṭaka)

Lesson 2
Dhammapada v. 393 I v. 80 I v. 277-9

Lesson 3
Dhammapada v. 60 I v. 387 I v. 18

Lesson 4
Milindapañha, 2.Chapter, 1. Question

Lesson 5
(continued) Milindapañha, 2.Chapter, 1. Question

Lesson 6
Mahāparinibbānasutta (Digha Nikāya 16)

Lesson 7
Mahāparinibbānasutta (Digha Nikāya 16)

Lesson 8
Mahāparinibbānasutta (Digha Nikāya 16) I Saṃyuttanikāya (XXII,94)

Lesson 9
Mahāparinibbānasutta (Digha Nikāya 16) I Udāna III, 10 I Udāna VII, 2

Lesson 10
Dhammacakkapavattanasutta (Saṃ. V, 420)

Index of Vocabular

A

B

C

V

Y

Index of Grammar

Numbers refer to the appropriate lesson

Appendix A – South East Asian Pali Alphabets

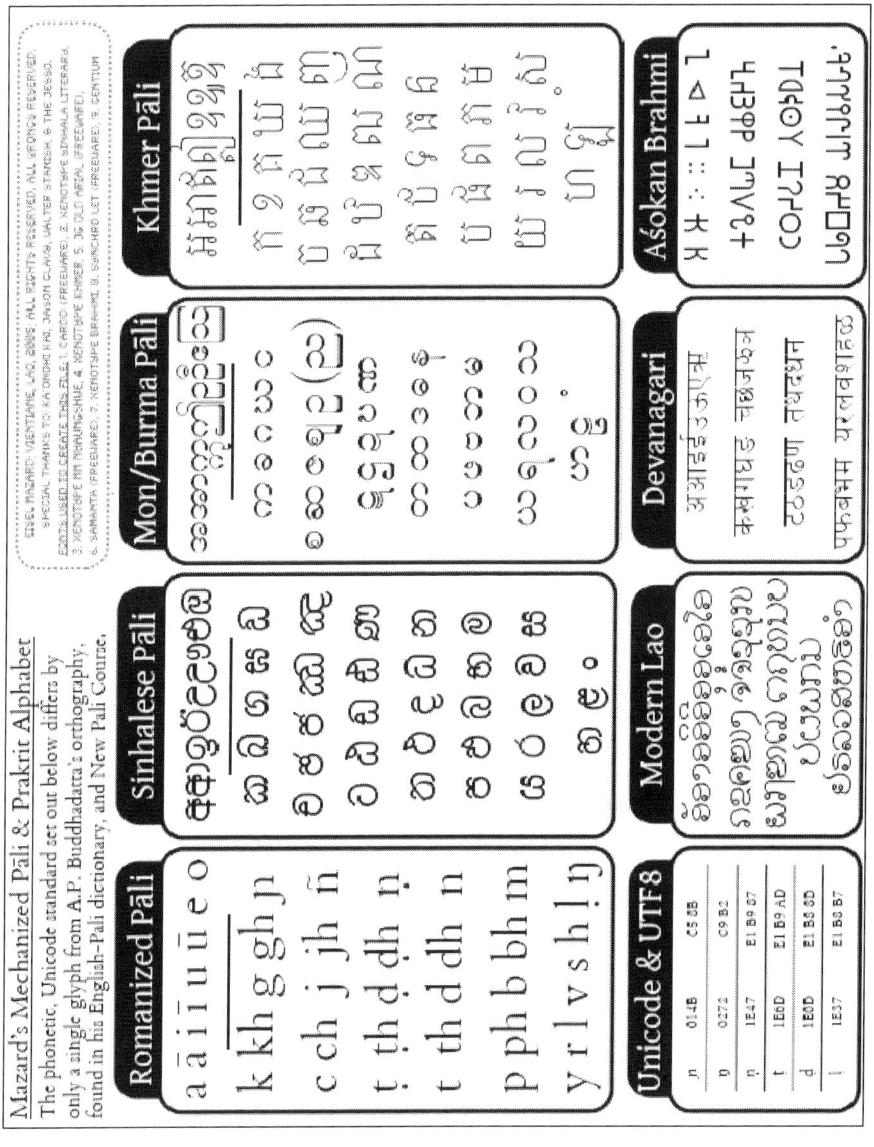
Mazard's Mechanized Pāli & Prakrit Alphabet
The phonetic, Unicode standard set out below differs by only a single glyph from A.P. Buddhadatta's orthography, found in his English-Pali dictionary, and New Pali Course.
Romanized Pāli
a ā i ī u ū e o
k kh g gh ṅ
c ch j jh ñ
ṭ ṭh ḍ ḍh ṇ
t th d dh n
p ph b bh m
y r l v s h ḷ ṃ
Sinhalese Pāli
Mon/Burma Pāli
Khmer Pāli
Unicode & UTF8
Modern Lao
Devanagari
Aśokan Brahmi

Appendix B – Grammar Basics[5]

What Are These Grammatical Concepts I've Got to Learn?

This is the easy part.

In what follows, I'm going to introduce you to the main concepts and explain them. If you read them with perfect comprehension, it will help you understand the grammatical concepts used in this book.

First Concept: Noun Cases

In English, it is the order of words in a sentence that tells you what their grammatical function is. Example:

The teacher gives a book to the student.

If you know even a little bit about English grammar, you will be able to say that the verb in this sentence is "gives." (It's the "action" word.) And once you've found the action word, the grammar of the rest of the sentence can be figured out by seeing how everything else relates to the action.

[5] Case introduction by Prof. Dowling adjusted for Pāli

In this sentence, for instance, you can easily see that "the teacher" is the *subject* of the verb. (It's the teacher who's "doing the giving.") In the same way, you can see that "the book" is the *direct object* of the verb. (The book is what's being given.) You can then see that "the student" is the *indirect object* of the verb. (It's the student to whom the book is being given.)

Don't just rush past my explanations. Go back and read over the previous two paragraphs if you didn't understand them completely. The grammatical concepts I'm presenting here are very simple, but if you don't understand them completely, you won't understand the related Pāli concepts I'm about to explain.

Verb = "action word." Subject = "doer of the action." Direct Object = "object of the action." Indirect Object = "recipient or beneficiary of the action." Okay?

I said that in English and the other modern European languages, it is word order that determines grammatical function. Look what happens when we invert the word order of the sample sentence:

The student gives a book to the teacher.

Watch very closely what's going on here. Note that "the student" is spelled just the same here as it was in the earlier sentence. So is "the teacher." The point is that *neither word has changed its form*. All we've done is move "student" up to the front of the sentence and put "teacher" at the end.

But now, to a speaker of English, the whole meaning has changed: it's the student who's doing the giving and the teacher who's doing the receiving of the book. (In grammatical terms, "the student" has become the subject of the sentence and "the teacher" has become the indirect object.)

Do English words ever change their form to indicate a change in meaning?

Yes.

Consider the following:

I *bring* my lunch to school on Thursdays.

I *brought* my lunch to school last Thursday.

The change from *bring* to *brought* signals, in English, a change from the present tense of the verb to the past tense. *Bring* is what is called a "strong verb." It's left over from an earlier stage of English when many more words changed their form -- that is, changed the way they were pronounced and spelled -- bring/brought -- to indicate a change in grammatical function.

When a language has a lot of words that change their actual form to signal a change in grammatical function, that language is said to be "highly inflected."

In a highly-inflected language, words mainly show their grammatical function by their form -- that is, you can tell just by looking at the word in isolation what role it plays in the sentence: you don't need word order to tell you -- and so word order doesn't mean as much when you're trying to figure out grammatical function.

This is an important concept, so make sure you're following everything here. In the sentences

The teacher gives a book to the student.

and

The student gives a book to the teacher.

there is simply no way to tell whether "teacher" and "student" is the subject of the verb or the indirect object of the verb without looking at the whole sentence.

Just seeing

the teacher

in isolation gives you no grammatical information at all.

By contrast, in the few cases where English keeps some of its earlier inflections, you don't need a whole sentence to tell you what grammatical function the word is fulfilling. For instance, if you just see

bring

and

brought

sitting there alone on the page, you can say that *bring* is present tense and *brought* is past tense.

In Pāli, practically every word in a sentence tells you its grammatical function by its form. Consider this sentence:

Ācariyo deti potthakam sissato.

Translation: "The teacher gives a book to the student."

For a number of reasons, that's not a very good Pāli sentence, but I want to use it to make a point. The point is this: to someone who reads Pāli, the form of "ācariyo" says that "ācariyo" is the subject of the verb. (It is the "ācariyo" who is "doing the giving" here.)

In the same way, "potthakam" shows by its form that it is the direct object of the verb. (The "potthakam" is what the ācariyo is giving.)

And finally, "sissato" shows by its form that it is the indirect object of the verb. (It is the "sissato" who is getting the *potthakam* from the *ācariyo*.)

Here comes the important part. ***Because each of these nouns shows its grammatical function by its form, that function doesn't change even when you switch the word order around in the sentence.***

Remember how we reversed the meaning of

The teacher gives a book to the student.

just by reversing the word order?

The student gives a book to the teacher.

In Pāli, you can put the words of our example sentence in virtually any order you want, and the *ācariyo* keeps on being the person who is doing the giving,
the *potthakam* keeps on being the object that is given, and the *sissato* keeps on being the person who is being given the book.

For purely stylistic reasons, some of the following are sentences no writer of "good" Pāli would ever construct, but in purely grammatical terms they all mean exactly the same thing:

Ācariyo deti potthakam sissato.
Potthakam sissato ācariyo deti.
Sissato potthakam ācariyo deti.
Deti sissato ācariyo potthakam.
(etc.)

It gets clumsy after a while to have to keep on saying that "the nouns in the sentence above retain their grammatical function so long as they retain the same form," so grammarians invented a shorthand way of saying the same thing. To say what grammatical function a Pāli noun shows by the form in which it is written, you simply mention the *case* of the noun.

This is the main "new" grammatical concept you're going to have to learn to study Pāli. When you memorize Pāli nouns -- and, as you'll see, adjectives, which have to "agree with" the nouns they modify -- what you really memorize is the cases through which each noun shows its grammatical function in a sentence.

Second concept: the nominative

This is easy. A noun occurs in the nominative case when it is the subject of the verb. In the sentence

Ācariyo deti potthakam sissato.

it is the nominative form of *ācariyo* that tells you that the *ācariyo* (teacher) is doing the giving here.

Every case comes in two "numbers," the singular and the plural. Don't let this perplex you. It just means that sometimes the form of the noun shows you that one person or thing is involved, and at other times it shows you that more than one person or thing is involved. Examples:

Ācariyo deti potthakaṃ sissato.
Ācariyā denti potthake sissatānam.

In the second sentence, I've put all the nouns into the plural number. Each noun is in the same case, so the meaning of the sentence stays the same: something is being given by someone to someone else. But in the first sentence it is a single *teacher* who is giving a single *book* to a single *student*. In the second sentence it is two or more *teachers* who are giving two or more *books* to two or more *students*.

Here's some grammatical jargon that I want you to make sure you understand. Don't go on until you're absolutely sure you understand what I'm saying about the two sentences above: 1) In the first sentence "ācariyo" is in the *nominative singular*. 2) In the second sentence, "ācariyā" is in the *nominative plural*.

Do you understand that? *Nominative* means, in both sentences, that the noun is showing by its form that it is the subject of the verb. Singular means that the sentence is talking only about a single "ācariyo." *Plural* means that there are two or more *ācariyā* giving away books.

Third concept: Accusative and Dative Case

Now I'm going to speed things up a bit.

Here are some more things you can say about the two sentences above: 1) In the first sentence, "potthakam" is in the *accusative singular*. 2) In the second sentence, "potthake" is in the *accusative plural*. 3) In the first sentence, "sissato" is in the *dative singular.* 4) In the second sentence, "sissatānam" is in the *dative plural.*

Do you see what's going on here? The *accusative* is the Pāli case that shows that a noun is the direct object of the verb. (The books are the "things being given" in these sentences.)

The *dative* is the Pāli case that shows that a noun is the indirect object of the verb. (The students are the ones "to whom the books are being given" in both sentences.)

The accusative singular shows that only one book is being given. The dative singular shows that only one student is getting or receiving the book. The accusative plural shows that two or more books are being given. The dative plural shows that two or more students are getting the books.

When you get farther along with Pāli, you'll learn that cases like the Accusative and the Dative have other uses as well, but these are the ones you want to start with.

Fourth Concept: the Genitive Case

This one is easy too.

The genitive case in Pāli usually signals some idea of possession. Somebody or something owns or possesses something else. Here are a couple of simple examples in English of how the genetive works:

The boy's hat was bright red.
The roof of the house was made of tile.
The teacher's book is large.

Now look at the last of these sentences. I'm about to give you the same sentence in Pāli. Here it is:

Potthakam ācariyassa mahantakam hoti.

As always, it is the *form* of the noun that tells you what the grammatical function is. In technical terms, you only have to say that "ācariyassa" in the sentence above is in the genitive case, and to understand what that means all you have to understand is that the book belongs to the teacher.

Fifth Concept: the Ablative, Instrumental and Locative Case

The ablative, instrumental and locative are the hardest Pāli cases to get an "intuitive" feel for, because the Indians at the time of the Buddha used the ablative, instrumental and locative for all sorts of different grammatical purposes.

Here's the easiest way to make sense of the ablative, instrumental and locative. In Pāli, these three cases tend to do the work that we do in English with common prepositions (*from, of, on, with, by, on account of, for, near, regarding,* etc).

Each of these little words signals some sort of relation between the noun and something else. For instance, you can say

The teacher puts the book *on* the shelf.

Here, the relation signalled by the preposition *on* is spatial: when the action is complete, one object (a book) is on top of another object (a bookshelf) as a result.

This is exactly what happens with the locative in Pāli. Here's the same sentence in Pāli with "bookshelf" (bhittiphalaka) in the ablative:

Ācariyo potthakaṃ bhittiphalak*e* thāpeti.

If you just basically concentrate on this idea, and then extend what you have understood to all the other common prepositions in English (again: *from, on, in, with, by*, etc), you'll never have trouble with the ablative, instrumental or locative in Pāli.

The key is this: when you see an ablative in a Pāli sentence, ask yourself what *relation* it is trying to signal between the noun in the ablative case and everything else in the sentence. Try first "*from, away from*" for the ablative and "*with, through, by means of*" with the instrumental. For the locative try "*in, on*". Then you will figure out its meaning "intuitively."

Here is a warning. The ablative/instrumental/locative has so many common uses in Pāli that grammarians have figured out names for a lot of them.

It is still customary in some Pāli courses to try to get students to understand the ablative/instrumental/locative by teaching them these categories.

My advice: forget the categories. They'll just confuse you, mainly because they get you worrying about non-essential secondary categories when what you want to know is what this ablative/locative *means* in this sentence.

When you're reading your *Pāli, the Buddhas Language* chapters, just go with the flow: learn the ablatives/locatives as they come up in the reading, and forget about fancy names for what they are doing.

In the end, you'll have learned all the categories, but without confusing yourself. (Once you've learned how these cases "work" in its various uses, you can go and get a grammatical table and learn the categories in 10 minutes. "Oh," you say to yourself, "that use is called 'the ablative of the place from which'!" But the important thing is that you were already understanding what it meant.)

Sixth Concept: Adjective Cases

This isn't really a new concept, but I'm putting it under a separate heading to emphasize that you've got to learn adjectives separately from nouns.

The key "concept" is this: adjectives have to agree with the nouns they modify in number and case. That sounds hard. In fact, it's incredibly easy. Start with *modify*.

You may remember from grade school that adjectives are words that give you new information about nouns. The grammarians' way of saying this is to say that the adjective "modifies" the noun. So:

The teacher had a book.

All you know about the book at this point is, so to speak, that it is a book (i.e., a rectangular object containing print and able to be read by those who understand the language in which it is printed).

But when you add adjectives to the sentence, you begin to get more specific ideas about the book:

The teacher had a large book.
The teacher had a large, old, dusty book.
The teacher had a large, old, dusty, difficult book.

In each of these instances, you say that an adjective ("large," "old," "dusty," "difficult") is adding something new to ("modifying") your idea of the book owned by the teacher.

The point about numbeThe point about number and case simply means that adjectives in Pāli have to be singular when the noun is singular, plural when the noun is plural, and display by their form the same grammatical function as the noun they are modifying:

Potthakam mahantam hoti. (This is a large book.)
Potthake mahante honti. (These are has [some] large books.)

The great news about adjectives is that they all have the same endings as one of the noun declensions you will already have learned. You do have to learn that adjectives belong to different declensions, but their forms are ones you'll already know from having memorized the noun declensions earlier.

Seventh Concept: Verb Tense and Mood

I'm not going to give you examples of Pāli tenses and moods, but I want to remind you of what tense and mood are before you start memorizing Pāli verb tables.

Tense just means that the form of a verb tells you the *time* in which the action described by the verb took place:

I *brought* my friend a book. (past tense)
I *bring* my friend a book. (present tense)
I *will bring* my friend a book (future tense)

In both English and Pāli, verb tenses allow speakers and writers of the language to do wonderfully complicated things, and these things all have complicated names in the grammar books.

Look at the shifts of time implied by the verbs in this sentence, for instance:

By the time you finish your study of *Pāli, the Buddhas Language*, you will have been one of the most conscientious readers ever to have started the study of Pāli this way.

Do you see what the verb lets the sentence do there? It takes the reader all the way up into a future state of affairs and lets them look back at it as a completed action or event.

Complicated tenses like that have complicated names (in both English and Pāli), and these you do have to learn. But if you get the idea of each tense before you start learning, you will never have any trouble remembering what each one does.

And Pāli verbs and Pāli verbs "behave" in wonderfully symmetrical ways: they are easy to memorize once you get a feel for how each tense is behaving. (This is impossible to explain ahead of time. You'll see what I mean when you start memorizing your verb tables.)

Eigth Concept: Verb Voice

The voice of a verb is either active or passive. The best way to understand this concept is to go look it up in a freshman comp book if you've forgotten. Here is the principle:

Active: John cooked the rice.
Passive: The rice was cooked by John.

Got it? Roughly speaking, the active voice signals that a person is performing or carrying out an action. The passive voice puts the object of the verb up into the subject position and says that the action was done "to" it: "The turkey was cooked by John."

Ashokan Inscription, Girnar India

Closest of all Ashokan inscriptions to canonical Pali, over 2300 years old

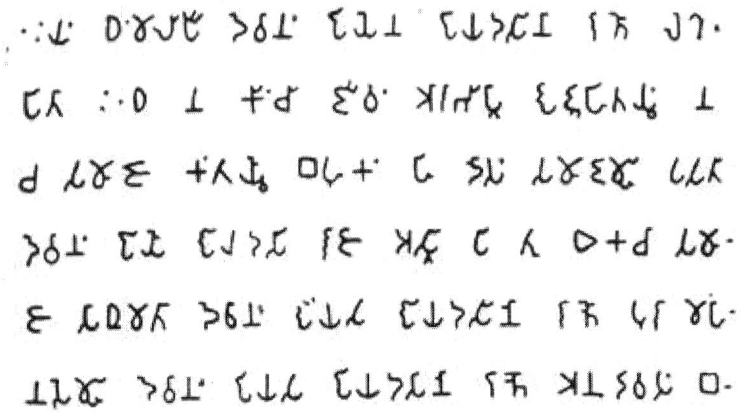

Transliteration (G b)

1. ...iyaṃ dhammalipī devānaṃ piyena piyadasinā raññо lekha-
2. pitā: idha na kañci jīvaṃ arabhittā paju hitavyaṃ na
3. cha samaje katavyo bahukaṃ hi dosaṃ samājamhi padati
4. devānaṃ piyo Piyadasi raja asti pi-tu ekachā samā
5. jā sadhumatā devānaṃ piyasa Piyadasino raño purā mahā
6. nase jamā devānaṃ piyasa Piyadasino raño anudivasaṃ ba-

....

Excerpt from the Udāna (bilingual study edition)

4.6 Piṇḍolasuttaṃ

4.6 Pindola

Evaṃ me sutaṃ Thus have I heard. **ekaṃ samayaṃ** On a certain occasion **BHAGAVĀ sāvatthiyaṃ viharati** the Blessed One dwelt at Savatthi **jetavane** in the Jeta forest **Anāthapiṇḍikassa ārāme** in the park of Anâthapindika. **Tena kho pana samayena** Now at that time **āyasmā piṇḍolabhāradvājo** the venerable Pindolabharadvâja **bhagavato avidūre nisinno hoti** was sitting, not far from the Blessed One **pallaṅkaṃ ābhujitvā** in a cross-legged position, **ujuṃ kāyaṃ paṇidhāya** with body erect. **āraññiko** He was a frequenter of forests, **piṇḍapātiko** a recipient of alms, **paṃsukūliko** a weaver of clothes made of rags taken from a dust-heap, **te-cīvariko** possessor of the three garments of a monk, **appiccho** content with little, **santuṭṭho** satisfied, **pavivitto** solitary, **asaṃsaṭṭho** living apart from men, **āraddhavīriyo** strenuous and eager **dhutavādo** a promoter of the ascetic exercises **adhi-cittam-anuyutto** and addicted to (states of) a higher mind.

Addasā kho BHAGAVĀ And the Blessed One beheld **āyasmantaṃ Piṇḍolabhāradvājaṃ** beheld the venerable Pindolabharadvâja, **avidūre nisinnaṃ** sitting not far off, **pallaṅkaṃ ābhujitvā** in a cross-legged position, **ujuṃ kāyaṃ paṇidhāya** with body erect. **āraññiko** He was a frequenter of forests, **piṇḍapātiko** a recipient of alms, **paṃsukūliko** a weaver of clothes made of rags taken from a dust-heap, **te-cīvariko** possessor of the three garments of a monk, **appiccho** content with little, **santuṭṭho** satisfied, **pavivitto** solitary, **asaṃsaṭṭho**

living apart from men, **āraddha-vīriyo** strenuous and eager **dhuta-vādo** a promoter of the ascetic exercises **adhi-cittam-anuyutto** and addicted to (states of) a higher mind.

Atha kho BHAGAVĀ And the Exalted One **etam'atthaṃ viditvā** in this connection **tāyaṃ velāyaṃ** on that occasion **imaṃ udānaṃ udānesi** – breathed forth this solemn utterance:–

"Anūpavādo anūpaghāto,
"To speak no ill, to injure not,
pātimokkhe ca saṃvaro;
To be restrained according to the precepts
Mattaññutā ca bhattasmiṃ,
To be temperate in food
pantañca sayanāsanaṃ;
To sleep secluded
Adhicitte ca āyogo,
To be dedicated to higher states of mind
etaṃ buddhāna sāsanan"ti.
This is the dispensation of the Awakened Ones.

Excerpt from the Milindapanho, (bilingual study edition)

7. Yonisomanasikārapañho

Rājā āha The king said: **"bhante nāgasena, yo na paṭisandahati,** 'Nâgasena, he who escapes rebirth **nanu so**

yoniso manasikārena na paṭisandahatī''ti? is it by direct attention that he escapes it?'

''Yoniso ca mahārāja, manasikārena paññāya ca aññehi ca kusalehi dhammehī''ti. 'Both by wisdom and direct attention, your Majesty, and by other good qualities.'

''Nanu, But are not **bhante, yoniso manasikāro yeva paññā''ti?**' direct attention and wisdom surely much the same?'

''Na hi, mahārāja, 'Certainly not. **añño manasikāro, aññā paññā,** Direct attention is one thing, wisdom another. **Imesaṃ kho, mahārāja, ajeḷaka-goṇa-mahiṃsa-oṭṭhagadrabhānami** Sheep and goats, oxen and buffaloes, camels and asses **manasikāro atthi** have attention**, paññā pana but wisdom** but wisdom **tesaṃ natthī''ti**, they have not.' **''Kallosi, bhante nāgasenā''ti.**'Well put, Nâgasena!'

Milindapañho

Pali - English Bilingual Study Edition

By Ven Bhikkhu Nagasena

The Milindapañho or "Questions of Milinda" is a Buddhist text which dates from approximately 100 BCE. It records a dialogue in which the Indo-Greek king Menander I (Milinda in Pali) of Bactria, who reigned in the second century BCE, poses questions on Buddhism to the sage Nagasena.

This unique study edition contains the English translation side by side the original Pali text. This allows any reader to casually read the text while improving their fundamental understanding of some of the most important Buddhist concepts through the eyes of the original text and Ven. Nagasenas unmatched witty replies.

Publication Date:	Dec 11 2009
ISBN/EAN13:	1449944787 / 9781449944780
Page Count:	166
Binding Type:	US Trade Paper
Trim Size:	5.5" x 8.5"
Language:	English
Color:	Black and White
Related Categories:	Religion / Buddhism / Theravada

Udana

Pali - English Bilingual Study Edition

Authored by Buddha Gotama

The Udana, the third book of the Khuddaka Nikaya, offers a rich collection of short suttas, each of which culminates in a short verse uttered by the Buddha.
Altogether there are eighty suttas, arranged in eight vaggas, or chapters.
The Udana contains important Suttas dealing with the concept of Nibbana and Insight Meditation. It is also from here that the famous simile of the blind men and an elephant found its way into world literature.
This unique bilingual study edition contains an English translation alongside the original Pali text. This allows any reader - even without knowing Pali - to casually read the text while deepening their fundamental understanding of some of the most important Buddhist concepts in the Buddha's own words.

Publication Date:	May 01 2010
ISBN/EAN13:	1452894736 / 9781452894737
Page Count:	276
Binding Type:	US Trade Paper
Trim Size:	5.5" x 8.5"
Language:	Pali
Color:	Black and White
Related Categories:	Religion / Buddhism / Theravada

36280695R00079

Printed in Great Britain
by Amazon